"In Debra's brilliant book of stories, she walks you through her writing journey and encourages you to overcome the obstacles and distractions of life to find time to tell your story. Read this book and get one step closer to your goal."
—Kary Oberbrunner, Author of *Day Job to Dream Job,*
Your Secret Name, and *The Deeper Path*

"Life brings many distractions, diversions and difficulties and we navigate them, creating new stories, while still hanging onto our dreams. Each event adds a beautiful piece to the whole picture. Debra's stories about her own life are filled with interesting ways she has remained true to her love of writing and are a great reminder for us not to wait till 'someday' but to forge ahead with the end in sight."
—Dan Miller, Author of *48 Days to the Work You Love*
—Joanne Miller, Author of *Creating a Haven of Peace*

"I have known Debra for over twenty years, and three characteristics have stood the test of time: faith, resolve, and an unfailing tenacity to chase her dreams. She has had the amazing ability to wear army boots, ice skates, baseball cleats, corporate pumps, and dancing shoes—each with the same amazing quality of grace and grit. And she wields her writer's pen with that same grace and grit as she tells real life stories and lessons learned.

In Exodus 4:2 (KJV), God asks Moses, 'What is that in thine hand?' If God were to ask Debra that question, the answer would be 'a pen.' And with that pen, faith, and resolve, Debra has written her way to her dreams. May you be inspired as you read to ask yourself this same question, 'What is that in thine hand?' And may you be prompted to do that thing you are compelled to do, no matter the challenges or curve balls life may throw at you."
—Brenda J. Dunagan, CEO, Dunagan and Associates LLC

"It takes a great storyteller to grab a reader's attention and change how they've perceived events in their own life. Debra's thoughtful and entertaining style of storytelling about events in and around her life's journey does just that. Her candid stories of overcoming adversities are laced with joy, determination, and gratitude. She teaches us that meaningful and joyful moments occur in our lives every day, even when things sometimes don't go our way."

—Al Simmons, Senior Financial Advisor, Wells Fargo

"Weaving memories and words in such a way only the great storytellers master, Debra Irene's reflections take you on a delightful journey of growth and rebirth, dreaming dreams then waking up to bigger ones. Filled with humor, anecdotes, and lovely lessons on life, you won't want to miss this read."

—Erika Beebe, Short Story Author of
"The Wheat Witch" and "Stage Fright"

Someday
I Will Write

Avava,

Thank you for your
special ministry,

Carry on —

Debra
Irene

Also by Debra Irene

Reflections

Helen's Heritage

Someday I Will Write

An Uncommon Journey to Finding
Time to Tell Your Stories, Finish Your Book,
and Fulfill Your Dream

DEBRA IRENE

AUTHOR ACADEMY elite

Printed in the United States of America

Published by Author Academy Elite
P.O. Box 43, Powell, OH 43035

www.AuthorAcademyElite.com

Cover images and author photos: Mark McDonald Photography, used by permission.

Interior photographs used by permission from the author's family collection.

Poem in Chapter 2 used by permission of Stephanie Coleman Bradshaw.

All Scripture quotations, unless otherwise indicated, are taken from the Holy Bible, New International Version®, NIV®. Copyright ©1973, 1978, 1984, 2011 by Biblica, Inc.™ Used by permission of Zondervan. All rights reserved worldwide. www.zondervan.com. The "NIV" and "New International Version" are trademarks registered in the United States Patent and Trademark Office by Biblica, Inc.™

This book is a work of non-fiction. Unless otherwise noted, the author and the publisher make no explicit guarantees as to the accuracy of the information contained in this book, and in some cases, names of people and places have been altered to protect their privacy.

Because of the dynamic nature of the internet, any web addresses or links contained in this book may have changed since publication and may no longer be valid. The views expressed in this work are solely those of the author and do not necessarily reflect the views of the publisher.

Paperback ISBN: 978-1-64085-779-7
Hardcover ISBN: 978-1-64085-780-3
Electronic ISBN: 978-1-64085-781-0

Library of Congress Control Number: 2019909775

to my three sons
and their children
and their children's children

*There is a time for everything,
and a season for every
activity under the heavens:*

—Ecclesiastes 3:1

Table of Contents

Part Two: A Time to Hope and a Time for Faith

Part Three: A Time for Family

Part Four: A Time to Let Go

Part Five: A Time to Work and a Time to Play

Foreword

My interaction with Debra Irene dates back ten years when I was a short-term employee at the office where she was employed. It was then Debra told me she wanted to write. I had seen her in action and, clearly, she was reliable. Her word was golden. Knowing she wouldn't be just another "writer wannabe," I asked her to join a writer's group that met at my home. Her writing was not strong in the beginning and we were unmerciful in our critiques. A lesser person would have quit. Now, I wish I could write like the stylist she has become.

Written over a period of several years, Debra Irene's story collection feels as if each piece has been seasoned and tenderized by the passage of time, like a good meal simmered in a slow cooker. The ingredients are abundant, organic in nature, gathered from everyday living and folded into warm-hearted prose to comfort and soothe or make us laugh or teary-eyed ... to help us understand who we are and how family, food, faith, friendship, and sportsmanship nourish and enrich.

In *Someday I Will Write*, themed stories are a reverent homage to small moments, morsels of time, like picking apples in the orchard on an autumn day ... cherishing notes her mother penciled on a lined tablet ... revisiting houses that once were home ... and a too-busy mom parking the car and taking her child to pet ponies on the opposite side of a fence—each memory infused with a subtle stop-and-smell-the-roses sensitivity.

Bringing clarity to the past and relevance to the present, sixty chapters form this signature collection, honoring an earnest promise, *Someday I Will Write.*

Martha McCarty, Author—*Five Island Diaries*

Preface

I was born into this world an introvert, timid with little self-confidence. I was afraid to speak for fear of saying something incorrect or that someone would make fun of my thoughts and words. Most times, I retreated to a private spot and wrote my thoughts and feelings down on paper. Sometimes I wrote poetry, especially if my feelings were hurt. Although I did not verbalize my feelings, I observed everything around me, especially the actions and interactions of other people, and I had a vivid memory and imagination. I looked into someone's eyes and heart and imagined a story based on things they said, their gestures, and their mannerisms. Also, I listened, observed, and was captivated with stories others would tell. How was I, this introvert, ever going to tell my own stories?

As I grew up and matured, I settled into analytical and administrative support work and raising a family with little thought about writing until I attended a children's literature festival in the mid-nineties with my oldest son. At first, the day-long trip to a small college campus a couple of hours from our home wasn't that appealing to me, but I had promised him I would attend this field trip and that he could bring a friend. The friend's mother came along too, so the four of us headed out in our red minivan for the day. Authors from all over the country were invited to present their work and interact with the young students and a few parents. I enjoyed listening to the stories of all of the authors we were assigned to see. One in particular made a lasting impression on me, a Missouri native—Clyde Robert Bulla (1914-2007). He primarily wrote children's western stories. He was gentle, soft spoken, and nearly eighty years old. While listening to him, something stirred deep within my heart. I wanted to pull him aside and pick his brain. I wanted to do what he was doing. I wanted to have a portfolio of books and speak to people about them, to autograph them and answer questions. But how was I going to accomplish this? I had not even begun to write. And what was I going to write about? How did he do this?

Instead, I returned to work the next day but had difficulty concentrating. I daydreamed about being an author. I remembered ideas and concepts I had as a child and teenager. I felt like my mother's family had an incredible history and a few remarkable stories that would make an awesome movie or book—our own version of *Roots*. I remembered a movie I watched in 1981 *(Rich and Famous)* about two friends with totally different writing styles and the funny storyline that went along with it. I was intrigued even though the movie was not critically acclaimed. It was about authors, so I remember it to this day.

I continued with my life surrounded by three sons and their activities until the youngest graduated from high school and went off to college, joining his brother. This would normally have been a time for me and, finally, my potential writing career. But due to a devastating divorce and having three sons in college, I found myself working at least seventy hours a week with little time to write. The desire to write prevailed through this time, and I had a concept for my first book, *Reflections*, a brief book of vignettes published in 2011. I began blogging, writing little heartfelt stories from years past and things that were going on in my present life, and I participated in a writers' group that met once a month. The gist of it: somehow, I made time to write and finish a book project, one of my life's dreams. During this project, I asked permission to use the name of a person mentioned in *Reflections*. My note to him began, "Someday I will write, someday when I have the time." My encourager and good friend said that I should hang onto that phrase. And so I have for almost a decade, knowing that some combination of those words would be the title of this book someday.

Someday I Will Write is a collection of my stories written over time—mostly over the past decade when there didn't appear to be time—when a demanding business career filled my days and I fought for a few hours in the evenings and on the weekends.

In *Someday I Will Write*, you will notice after each story I have described when the story was written and in some cases why it was written, or I might give you a little more insight into the story or the aftermath. You can see that I made the time to write, and so can you, my friend, if that is something you long to do. If you're reading for pleasure or a hobby, don't worry about needing hours to finish a segment. These stories are short and independent of each other. You can read a story or two as you have time and then toss the book aside for another day. The stories are not in chronological order but are grouped into five parts representing the different seasons and times in our lives.

During the time that many of these stories were written, I also finished telling my mother's life story for her. *Helen's Heritage* was published in 2016. That idea I had back as a teenager that our family stories could make a good book became a reality. Who knows, maybe it will be the basis for a movie someday too.

But for now, someday is today for *Someday I Will Write*. I hope you enjoy my stories.

Debra Irene

Introduction
A Dream and a Miracle

A storyteller of real-life adventures and everyday life—that's what I call myself. So, how did this all begin?

The year was 2010. I was working through the financial repercussions of a devastating divorce a few years earlier. I had two very good-paying jobs, one a career job, and three sons in college. Even though I worked about seventy hours a week, I managed to find a little time to devote to a lifelong dream of writing. I started one of my project ideas—a small book of vignettes reflecting on people in my life.

I was determined to complete the project despite my schedule. I had heard about self-publishing, and as I gazed out my condo window at a traditional publishing company in downtown Kansas City, I wondered about the best way to break into this world of publishing. So, I called a friend (Brenda) for advice. She confessed that she wasn't sure, but she knew someone who would know. She said I needed to attend his two-day writing seminar *(Write to the Bank)* in Franklin, Tennessee. This was, of course, impossible. Remember: I worked two jobs, was in a financial crisis, and this suburb of Nashville was 575 miles away.

Brenda said, "At least think about it."

I looked into airfare and hotel possibilities for two to three nights and knew that I would have to come up with the registration fee, which I believe was between $200-$300. I remember feeling overwhelmed with it all. Then another friend offered to drive for a little getaway if I was able to take off the time from work. I tucked that away in my memory bank as I pondered how to come up with the necessary funds.

One evening, I attended a business social event at a local Marriott hotel. The grand prize giveaway for the evening was 60,000 Marriott rewards points. As I signed my name on the strip of paper, I told our hostess that I needed to win the grand prize and jokingly asked if there was a Marriott in Franklin, Tennessee. She assured me there were a few nearby and throughout the evening told everyone I needed to win to go to Franklin, Tennessee. People laughed and wondered why anyone "needed" to go to—where? Yes, Franklin, Tennessee. At the end of the evening when the names were drawn, I watched as the third and second place winners claimed their prizes. Then, when the name was drawn for the grand prize, the hostess laughed and said, "She's going to Franklin, Tennessee!"

My friend, Brenda, smiled when I told her the Marriott story and encouraged me to wait and see if something else fell into place. Then, a week later, I was on a call with the administrator of my 401(k) plan at work. One of my sons needed an additional $3,000 for school that semester, and I investigated the possibility of withdrawing some of the money for educational purposes. After answering many questions and jumping through all the hoops, I found out our situation didn't qualify for that withdrawal. But the administrator said, "You do have a small amount from a previous rollover that you can withdraw without question." I was shocked to learn the amount was almost the exact amount needed to cover the registration fee for the writing seminar. That was the final piece. We had to find another avenue for the funds for my son, and I had to arrange for time away with my two employers. But I was going to Franklin, Tennessee!

And so, in September of 2010, I traveled from Kansas City to Franklin, Tennessee, for a writer's seminar and walked into a room full of extroverts and upbeat people who wanted to live *their* dreams. My goodness, all I wanted to do was figure out how to finish and publish a little book. I mostly listened to everyone else and the outstanding speakers.

I learned I needed to start a blog (something I told Brenda I would never do). I didn't have time to print and publish my own book like some planned to do. I barely had time to write. Furthermore, I knew that I could wait forever for a traditional publisher. Then an executive from Thomas Nelson spoke and mentioned that their new self-publishing division had teamed with *Women of Faith* for a writing contest where the winner would receive a free publishing package. That sparked my interest and I felt was the meant-to-be part of the program for me.

I returned home to Kansas City, wrote my first blog (with Brenda's encouragement), and contemplated how I was going to finish my manuscript by the contest deadline—only three months away. Brenda pointed out that my book was the style that didn't have a specific ending and that I should stop writing when I reached the minimum number of words (10,000). I could write a sequel later. What a tremendous piece of advice that was. After all, I wasn't writing a novel. That December, I took a week's vacation from my career job and devoted several hours each day to reach the minimum word count. I continued to work my supplemental night job, and by December 31, I was ready to push the button. I entered my little book of vignettes in the contest.

Although I did not win, I received a discount on a publishing package with WestBow Press for entering the contest and was able to purchase that package with an unexpected bonus in January. I watched the dream unfold, month by month, like

Brenda encouraged. And in April of 2011, I held my first copy of *Reflections*.

This was a very big deal to me, my own personal miracle. My mind was flooded with other book ideas. But the one that took front and center was a project for my mother. She wanted to tell her life story and had no idea what to do. She didn't have a concept, a format in mind. Neither did I at first. But we started writing it down little by little, and I kept blogging, telling my own stories. In the meantime, a few of my stories were published by *Farm & Ranch Living, Country, Country Extra,* and *The Missouri Golf Post.*

I continued with my career job but dreamed that someday writing could be my career. Five years later, I held my second published book *Helen's Heritage*—my mother's story, her dream. This was a project very near and dear to us. Not only is it my mother's life story, but it is a family documentary—a forty-thousand-word family history book filled with short stories and vignettes merged in with seventy-five images from about 1880 through today. In addition to that, I have enough blog material for another book when I am ready to compile it.

Someday, I *will* retire from that day job, but I can't imagine ever retiring from my dream of writing. There are more stories to tell and more projects to complete. A dream, a miracle (or two), and a *Brenda* in my life—those were the keys!

I first posted a version of this story as a blog within the 48 Days group as a note of appreciation to Dan and Joanne Miller. When the publisher of my first two books contacted me to write a blog for their website about my publishing experience, I had the perfect piece. They posted their version in the blog section of WestBow Press's website as a two-part series, the first in May 2017 and the second in June 2017. And now I *have* compiled all of that blog material mentioned above along with other short stories into this book—*Someday I Will Write.*

PART ONE

A Time to Remember

CHAPTER 1

Apple Time

I love this time of year, apple time.

For a day or two or three, I reminisce of other, less complicated, places and times. It all started over fifty years ago when I watched my grandmother peel apples to make an apple pie. Spellbound, I stared into the pan as the unbroken skin coils fell. Mammy convinced me the peeling was the best, most nutritious part of the apple. Throughout my childhood, I watched Mammy, my aunts, and my mother prepare delicious desserts from this red fruit—pies, cakes, cobblers, cinnamon apples, and jelly. And then there was *the recipe*, apple butter. I am fully aware that many families share in this fall tradition, each with their own unique method and recipe. I am right there with them as I boast yet refrain ever so slightly from "spilling the beans" ... the secret ingredient in our recipe. Of course, ours is the best. After all, people who say they don't like apple butter change their tune after tasting *the recipe*.

When I was a young mother of three little boys, I wanted to go back thirty years and relive those apple days. Baking an occasional apple pie didn't seem sufficient. I didn't want some of these other domestic skills (or in my opinion, this art) and *the recipe* to be forgotten. So, I asked my mother to locate the family recipe and to come and visit for a few days. She brought all the necessary equipment along with *the recipe*. I learned what made up a bushel and a half bushel of apples, became acquainted with a ricer and the manual work associated with it, and finally felt the satisfaction of hearing my jars filled with precious treasure seal with a ping. The day started early and ended late, but this craft has always been the most rewarding job I have ever known. What started as a novelty idea turned into my own ritual over the next several years in autumn. I made apple butter/apple jelly gift baskets as Christmas presents (the boys loved both), and somehow this annual tradition turned into fundraisers for church and little league baseball teams—bushels and bushels of apples—apple pies, apple butter, and apple jelly. Each year, we made a day trip to the orchard and sometimes actually picked the apples, what fun! I had a product that urban and suburban families enjoyed sharing with their family and friends.

It was, indeed, a great deal of work. After a decade of fundraising, my life evolved. The demanding corporate world left little time for this time-consuming craft. I simply no longer had the time. To the dismay of many, I mothballed the ricer my mother had given me.

Another decade passed, and life changed again. My youngest son headed off to college, and I prepared to move into smaller accommodations. I uncovered my ricer packed away deep in a closet. I could not bear to part with it. The desire to return to simpler times resurrected once again. That fall, I made a trip to the apple orchard I had visited annually all those years with my boys. I didn't recognize the vacant parking lot and almost missed the turn into the drive. The trees were bare, picnic tables were empty, and no one fried fritters in the kettle in the open pit. I felt like I was in a ghost town of an old western movie.

As I climbed the steps to the porch, I wondered if the little shop door would open. I peeked inside and heard someone say, "May I help you?"

"I hoped to buy some apples."

"That's all we have, number twos," she said as she pointed to ten half bushel sacks against the stairs. "It wasn't a good year. We had only one day of public picking."

Number twos were exactly what I needed, so I hauled five sacks to the register and glanced over at the shelf where a few jars of jelly and apple butter remained for sale. I asked her if they had made apple butter that year and learned the entire orchard was for sale. One thing hadn't changed. She accepted my personal check like she had ten years ago. I felt a bit numb as I pulled out of the drive, headed down the county road, and gazed at the beautiful colors—gold, yellow, orange, and chestnut—strewn through the rolling hills and countryside. Sorrow gushed from deep within my heart. I wanted to rescue the orchard, to care for it. I wondered if I could make a living at it. Could I live off the land? Was there any way to save it? I imagined hiring a team to help. We could work hard in the spring, summer, and fall, satisfied with the work of our hands, and then share the fruit of our labor with others. We could restore the hustle-bustle of the orchard shop in the fall, and then I could relax in the winter by the fire with my journal. Of course, I did not have the means to invest in such a project. And although I still had the skill to produce my family recipe, I doubted that I had the experience or expertise required to run an entire orchard. It was a fleeting thought, an impossible dream.

I headed back to the city and secretly made several batches of *the recipe,* which I unveiled that Christmas. Everyone was thrilled and amazed that I had accomplished the task. Although an empty nester, I was busy as ever. With two sons still in college, I worked two jobs and was in the final stages of writing a book. Some people suggested that I simplify the process, perhaps use a slow cooker or even buy applesauce instead of harvesting the pulp if I decided to make it the following year. But I could not bring myself to do that. I would do it the way I was taught or not do it at all. In many ways, it is therapeutic, and I feel I honor my heritage with this tradition.

So, this year I placed a call to the old familiar apple orchard only to hear, "The number you have dialed has been disconnected and is no longer in service." I didn't want to chance driving there. I knew in my heart it was gone, and I felt sad, very sad. But I did take a break from my hectic schedule and set out for a day trip to a small rural town's fall festival. With Main Street blocked off, craftsmen and women displayed their talents, entertainers performed on the courthouse steps, and yes, there were apples from a nearby orchard. This time I purchased a modest bushel. The next weekend, I unpacked my ricer one more time and returned to my roots. After a day of washing, coring, cooking, ricing, baking, and executing the delicate canning process, the smell of apples and cinnamon permeated the house. Two dozen pint-size jars filled with *the recipe* assumed the prestigious position of the sealed containers on the counter.

My body experienced a few more aches than it did that first year of apple butter time when I was thirty-something—stiff neck, sore feet, strained back. But as I headed up the stairs to bed that night, I heard the final jar on the windowsill ping, and somehow the aches didn't matter.

You know what? I think I smiled a little more that week. Perhaps I worked out a bit of stress, and my joy from completing a project the old-fashioned way brought a satisfaction that my laptop couldn't match. Yes, I think I'll have to keep that old ricer and the wooden mallet, too. And since confession is good for the soul, "Mammy, I have *spilled the beans* a time or two!"

A rural magazine held onto this story for over a year before sending me a rejection email after initially indicating they wanted to publish it. Then, a year later, a condensed version of my short story and blog "Apple Time" was published in the August/September 2014 issue of a different magazine, *Farm & Ranch Living*, titled "Apple Butter Time." The editor of the magazine wanted the family apple butter recipe to go along with their shortened story.

So, I reluctantly *spilled the beans* again to get paid for my first published story in a national magazine. The magazine had no problem disclosing the secret ingredient.

CHAPTER 2

A House, A Home

A house can be house, or a house can be a home. A house is made of wood, brick, or stone, but a home is made of memories, stories, and love. I am writing today about the latter—a home. I remember when I first met this home. It was my Aunt Lizzie and Uncle Hike's home.

I remember looking at this picture frequently growing up in California as Mother talked about the two of them. This picture was taken in the early days of their homeownership. They moved into their new house on New Year's Day, 1937. Over the next

twenty-five years, by the time I first visited, the two of them transformed this into a much-adored home.

When we moved to the Midwest in the mid-60s, this home became like my grandma's home. You see, Aunt Lizzie was my mother's oldest sister, who was twenty-nine years her senior. So, my Aunt Lizzie was more like "Grandma Lizzie." This was not like other houses we had left behind in modern southern California. It was located six miles into the country off the highway on a dirt road and up a rocky driveway.

There was a well a few feet from the back door that yielded fresh, cold water. I learned the meaning of "drawing water" as we lowered the bucket down into the well and pulled it back up by the attached rope.

There was an outhouse instead of a bathroom and a rooster who attacked you as you walked to the "facility." You had to run fast to protect your legs from his painful pecks. I don't know why he couldn't stay in the chicken coup and keep the hens happy. Which brings up another thing—eggs were collected from a real-life hen house rather than buying them at the grocery store.

Then there was the cow that Uncle Hike patiently tried to teach me to milk. I think her name was Bessie. I either didn't have the strength or didn't have the technique. But *he* always managed to fill the bucket full every morning and every night. He delivered it to Aunt Lizzie, who knew how to get the most out of each bucket. We had fresh whole cream for coffee, and she taught me to churn butter. Sometimes we had buttermilk, and in the summer, we made homemade ice cream.

After we milked the cow, we shucked corn so that mean old rooster and the hens would have something to eat. Sometimes I simply sat and watched Uncle Hike whittle away his worries. That wasn't something I saw in southern California, either.

Each year, Uncle Hike hid his watermelon patch to keep the brazen teenagers from vandalizing it. He would say, "You know, I wouldn't care if they only took a watermelon and ate it." But they made a game of it to find the patch and destroy every melon—not funny.

I remember that I tagged along on strolls of the property and neighboring property to search for arrowheads. Occasionally we found one, but I think Uncle Hike had already confiscated most of them judging from the number he had mounted in frames all over the walls of the home.

When we returned, I helped Aunt Lizzie prepare lunch, and then she showed me how to make a peach or apple pie from scratch. But my favorite thing to do with her was to wake up early before anyone else and help her fix breakfast for everyone who had slept over the night before—biscuits, gravy, eggs, pancakes, sausage, bacon—the works. She did most of the fixing, and I usually set the table—and what a beautiful table she could spread. Uncle Hike had his special spot at the table with plenty of room to "hike" one leg up on the chair, rest his elbow on it, and perch his coffee in the same hand. (Have you figured out how he acquired his nickname?)

A brisk breeze blew in from the bedroom and made up for the lack of air conditioning. After dark you could hear June bugs slam against the screens, crickets chirp, and various other critters that I could never identify. And, of course, in the morning, we awakened to the crow of that aggressive rooster and the elegant singing of the birds. Uncle Hike taught me to listen to one in particular whistling "Wet year, wet year," announcing it would rain that day.

Please don't mistake the lack of a few modern conveniences as uncomfortable. Aunt Lizzie decorated beautifully and kept the home spotless. I loved her white curtains. Flowers and shrubs were abundant in the yard close to the home. She was the epitome of Proverbs 31.

Many of these reflections were created with others. You see, I spent most of my time there on the weekends traveling up from Arkansas with my mother and sisters, and my cousin Lee (more like "Uncle Lee") brought his family down from Kansas City. We all converged there for the weekends until we all ultimately moved to the area—about the time there was much excitement with plans for indoor plumbing, running water, and a bathroom for the home.

I have shared my memories, but everyone in my extended family could write *their* memories because Aunt Lizzie was mother, grandma, great-grandma, aunt, and great-aunt to many. It was the place to go for Easter, Fourth of July, Memorial Day, and any and every ordinary day—no need for notice to drop in.

There was so much life in that home, and as goes the circle of life, so there was death. This home that brought so much life to our family was the passing place for some as well—Auntie (our matriarch, Aunt Myrt, Grandpa's sister), Uncle Hike's sister, my grandma (Rhoda Margaret "Mag"), and finally Uncle Hike. They were brought "home" to transition to their heavenly home.

After Uncle Hike passed away and Aunt Lizzie moved into town, Cousin Lee and his friendly wife, Charlene, moved into the homestead. She made *everyone* feel loved and special. They carried on many of the same traditions with their family. Charlene continued to make this house a home after Aunt Lizzie and Lee both passed on. It became "Granny's house" to her grandchildren and great-grandchildren. Every Sunday her entire family converged the way we had forty years ago and three generations earlier.

Then, without warning, one year ago Granny slipped away from us … such unexpected loss and sorrow. The family still assembles, seeking that at-home comfort and security. They gather on Sundays clinging to that home—the memories, the love, the unity. And I wonder who will make memories for the next generation. As the lights are turned off, will we hear, "Good night, Grandpa, good night, Grandma, good night, Sister?"

And you thought that originated with *The Waltons*? Nope—that was my cousin Rita!

Turn off the lights … lock the door.
No one lives here anymore.
No more kisses … no more hugs.
No more spoken words of love.
Tears start falling … one by one.
Trying not to come undone.
Whisper good-bye … shut the door.
No one lives here anymore.

—Stephanie Coleman Bradshaw
(4th Generation)

The home awaits the next generation.

A condensed version of this blog (originally written in October of 2011) was published in the August/September 2016 issue of *Country* magazine as "Heart of a Home." My extended family loved seeing this in a national magazine, and many had similar recollections. My third cousin Stephanie (Aunt Lizzie's great-granddaughter) wrote the poem around the same time that I wrote this story. It was a perfect piece to add at the end.

CHAPTER 3

Another House, Another Home

It was important to me to arrive before dark. I pulled into the driveway around 5:00 p.m. on a mild but breezy day in early February. I glanced at the "For Sale" sign in the yard and pulled my scarf a little tighter around my neck as I walked down the sloping drive to the backyard. The chain-link gate was open wide, inviting me in.

It was hard to imagine that almost thirty-five years had passed since I saw the house for the very first time after dark on that October evening—that a lifetime had gone by, raising a family and growing older.

I looked over the familiar grounds and prayed for the new family that would come and restore the house ...

- that a spirit of unity would encompass every inch of the inside and the outside,

- that the plank on the step of the lower deck would be nailed down,

- that the football laying on top of the pool cover would sail through the air,

- that the cover would be removed and sparkling blue water would swirl in the pool,

- that someone would warm up for baseball games at the back fence,

- that a ball would once again roll around the rim of the hoop on the garage and fall through for a score,

- that there would be tinkering sounds in the garage,

- that hot dogs and burgers would sizzle on the grill,

- that a spunky young pup would dart back and forth between the fence on the property lines, not knowing his predecessor rests below,

- that little feet would chase fireflies as the sun went down,

- that a cord of wood would be stacked at the back door ready to warm the inside with a cozy fire, both upstairs and downstairs,

… and, oh, so much more.

I looked toward the barren woods at the back of the yard beyond the fence and remembered the beautiful green tree line in summertime, the Redbuds in springtime, and the rustling of many leaves in autumn that covered the grounds. There is so much that only I could tell someone about this house—like why the drive is gated, why there is a door underneath the deck, why the garage is detached, why that was changed, when that was installed. But none of those things really matter anymore. It will be a home where someone else will have their own whys and whens. There must be a family somewhere who needs this house and will make it a home.

I turned to walk back to the driveway and stopped at the side door of the garage. It was cracked open. The frame was worn. I could not bring myself to push the door open and walk inside. Instead, I strolled up the driveway to my car.

I doubt that anyone noticed my visit to the empty dwelling as I said goodbye, again, for the last time. I didn't peer inside the house, either.

I would never have guessed thirty-five years ago that this is the way I would bid farewell. I don't know what happened here the last few years, but I know what can happen in the years to come.

Family, come hither. This house is ready to say, *Welcome home.*

This was written and posted as a blog in February 2018. Someone commented, "There's a bit of mystique in this piece since you didn't reveal what had happened in the span of years between then and now." My response, "… that is a story for another time."

CHAPTER 4

The Tablet

I t wasn't an iPad, Galaxy, Nexus, or ZenPad.

In between household chores and taking care of four daughters, occasionally she took a break. She walked into the narrow galley kitchen, poured a cup of coffee, grabbed the tablet out of a drawer, and carried everything into the small dining room. She pulled out a chair and, with pen in hand, began her epistle. She dated them at the top—various months and years in the early 1960s. And then it was Dear Lizzie, Delta, Eunice, Wanda, Mil-

dred, or Lorraine—some of her sisters and sisters-in-law in the faraway land of Missouri. Oh, I had been there to visit when I was a baby. There were pictures of us—Mother, Sister Vickie, and me—at Uncle Marve and Aunt Wanda's Civil War-era farmhouse, but I simply could not remember meeting these relatives.

She wrote for fifteen or twenty minutes about what we were doing, how we were feeling, how other nearby family members were in case they had not had time to write—Elnora, Geneva, Clara, and Louise. She could easily write five or six pages on the 6 x 9 ruled paper. Sometimes she finalized the letter, and sometimes she finished in the next day or two, then placed the folded pages in a small envelope with a four-cent stamp and entrusted these precious words to the mailman to ensure they were delivered 1,700 miles away. In a few weeks, she received an envelope in return. Many times, she, my mother, read the replies to me which were written on the same type of tablet paper by her sisters.

Mother says my writing reminds her of Aunt Lizzie, and that makes me smile. She says Aunt Lizzie had a beautiful penmanship and was very detailed in her writing. She painted pictures with words of her rural life—like what flowers and shrubs were in bloom in her yard at the time (pink peonies, red roses, yellow tulips and daffodils, or lilac bushes)—or maybe she described the abundance from her garden that year and how big Uncle Hike's watermelons were. In other seasons, it might have been how deep the snow was. And, like Mother, she reported in on the entire family.

The first time that I can remember meeting Aunt Lizzie was when she came to California to visit her daughter, who owned a restaurant in town. I was at the restaurant waiting for my mother's shift to end, sitting at the snack bar. She walked in with several others, sat at a large round table, and called me over.

She gently squeezed me at the waist and said, "Honey, do you know who I am?"

I shook my head no.

"I'm your Aunt Lizzie. Your mother's oldest sister."

I was awestruck. This lady was no longer words on a tablet but a real, live person.

The tablet was useful for other things, too—grocery lists, reminders, figuring a budget, and writing down recipes—like Aunt Clara's cobbler, which was famously renamed *Clara's Clabbler* because of the spelling error when Clara wrote it down for Mother on the tablet. More than thirty years later, when I wanted the family apple butter recipe—you guessed it—I wrote it down on a tablet. Yes, I had a tablet, too, and needed the ruled pad to write straight. Even with the lines, I still managed to write crooked.

Mother had to re-write *Clara's Clabbler* when the original deteriorated with age and use. I opted to type the apple butter recipe a few years ago but have placed both of these handwritten recipes in a protective sleeve for future generations to appreciate. (I sure hope they do.)

We weren't the only ones who used a tablet. This past year, I came across a little treasure written in 1992 by my lifelong friend, Cheryl, who died way too young at the age of forty-eight, twelve years after penning the letter. I was so excited to find it—her very own words in her very own handwriting. It's like she was right there with me after all these years. I will keep it forever.

The art of handwriting a personal note seems to be a thing of the past. So, it pleases me when I receive one. The notes tell many stories beyond the words on the paper if you have a bit of imagination. Last summer, I lost another close friend, Cathy, unexpectedly. When visiting her condo the week after she passed, I came across a thank-you note from my sweet, new daughter-in-law and surmised from the smudge that Cathy must have been drinking her morning coffee when she read it. I then realized the art of a personal, handwritten note is not totally lost. My faith was restored.

What another treasure I had found. But how guilty I felt. Last Christmas, I had every intention of writing a note in a card to all of the generous people who came to the book signings for *Helen's Heritage*. I couldn't seem to find the time. I had every excuse under the sun—too busy, too stressed, overworked, no one really cares. Truth was, I didn't make the time. And so, this one who calls herself a writer will do better. I promise.

I haven't seen the tablet for a few years. I looked for one at the grocery store today. It took some digging, but I found one for $1.59—so little money but, oh, so much potential for brightening someone's day.

Maybe, yes maybe, someone will find a treasure from me someday.

A version of this blog written in April 2017 was published in the July 2017 issue of *Country Extra* magazine as "Handwritten Treasures." The magazine editor expanded the story to feature my mother and the book I wrote for her, *Helen's Heritage,* her life stories. We were grateful for the exposure.

CHAPTER 5

Aunt Elnora

S he wasn't very tall. She was round, full, robust. She was a "dark one." You see, of my mother's fifteen siblings, about half of them were like Mama, fair skinned with light hair and blue eyes (Grandma), and the other half had dark hair, some with brown eyes (Grandpa). Aunt Elnora had a gentle, quiet spirit but had a sense of humor, which she revealed to her inner family circle. She was my surrogate grandmother during my early childhood in California, although she was my aunt—my mother's second oldest sister of eight girls. She had one daughter about my mother's age (Geneva) and one grandson. She found the love of her life in her fifties. I remember being a little embarrassed when they kissed on our porch as I ran into the house with my cousins and friends. Today, I smile when I think of that and am glad that I witnessed their tender love—Newt and Elnora.

It irritated me that my best friend's mother kept saying her name wrong. Eleanor was that former president's wife's name. Many times I corrected her ... Elnora, Elnora, Elnora!

Her yard overflowed with flowers. When sisters and I spent the night, she prepared pancakes for breakfast. She made them tiny so that we could boast about how many we had eaten—maybe a dozen. Sister Vickie ate more. There were white and black rabbits in cages in her back yard. She let us pet them. Their fur was so, so soft. Our poodle Flip liked playing with her dog Alvin.

We moved far away—back to the family's hometown in Missouri—around more aunts, uncles, cousins, and Grandpa. Three years later she came to visit, the summer of 1968. She cooked for us once again even though Mama said she had not been feeling well. I remember having a discussion with my younger sister about age as we waited at the table. Kathy wanted to know if the age thirty was old. I said, "Yes." But before I could explain further, Aunt Elnora bustled through the doorway between the kitchen and dining room with a big bowl of mashed potatoes, set them on the table, and corrected me. "Why, no! Thirty's not old. I wish I was thirty." Yes, I did think Aunt Elnora was old. After all, she had been like my grandmother all those years in California since Grandma died when I was only three years old.

After she cooked, she also washed the dishes and then went in the living room and sat in the rocking chair. Mama said her bad heart drained her energy—a leaky valve which might have been caused from a childhood bout of rheumatic fever. *The Lawrence Welk Show* came on and someone sang "In the Garden." Aunt Elnora said, "That is my favorite hymn. I want someone to sing that at my funeral."

I remember thinking, "That's a nice song, but you're not *that* old yet." She stayed a few more days, then returned home on a bus to her life with her caring husband. They had moved to a duplex community where he worked as the caretaker.

A few weeks later, still in the heat of the summer—August 1—I asked Mama if I could sleep on the couch because it was so hot upstairs in my bedroom. Soon after Mama had climbed into bed, the telephone on the end table next to the couch where I lay rang. Mother could not understand why I would not answer it as she rushed into the living room and picked up the receiver. Mother listened as Aunt Clara said, "Hold on to your hats. I've got bad news."

I don't know why, but I already knew. As the story goes, Newt and Elnora had finished dinner and shared a laugh about eating a whole chicken—it was only a "little" chicken—then he left to lock up the laundry facilities. A neighbor saw Elnora come out of their house and look toward the laundry room as she fell on the sidewalk. She was already gone when Newt reached her, although she was transported by ambulance to the hospital in hopes of a miracle. But this was not the day for a miracle.

The family in Missouri made plans to travel for the funeral and burial, which would be in California. Aunt Eunice and Uncle Rube offered to take both of their vehicles, so I was privileged to go. After Kathy, Karin, and I climbed into the back of the station wagon, Grandpa reached for the door to shut it and said, "I should grab my bag and get in there with you." But he couldn't make the trip. He was eighty-eight and had outlived four of his sixteen children. We arrived at Geneva's house in the middle of the night. I visited cousins and a close friend from school. Then, in a couple of days, it was time for the funeral.

I was twelve years old. It was not my first funeral. I knew the drill—reading of the obituary, a song or two, a short message, and then the viewing. As the minister read the obituary, I recalled what she had said that evening in the rocker ... "In the Garden." Why didn't I tell someone? Well, she must have mentioned that to someone else as well, because when he was finished, a recording of a song began ... "I come to the garden alone..." And I breathed a sigh of relief. After the sermon, I stood alongside Mama in the family line. But when we were to move closer, I could not. Mama grabbed my waist to help me, but I said, "I can't." I stayed back as Mama stepped closer for one last goodbye. Aunt Elnora's hair had been permed since returning to California, and I wasn't sure they had the right person. Could there have been a mistake? I guess not, because we proceeded to the cemetery and laid her to rest.

Two score and four years have passed since that hot summer of 1968, and I don't know why Aunt Elnora is at the forefront of my mind and in my heart. Maybe it's because at my next birthday,

I will be the age she was at her death. I have missed her—we all have missed her—and I realize she really was not that old. But, like her, I have come to understand my mortality. I find myself thinking her same thoughts. I have asked my sisters, if I precede them in death, to please play "Give Me Jesus" by Fernando Ortega at my funeral.

One last thing: "Aunt Elnora, when my time comes, make sure you tag along with Grandpa and Grandma and escort me up that pearly white staircase or meet me at the top. It will be so good to see you."

This was written and posted as a blog in April 2013. I love and miss my Aunt Elnora and her daughter, my "Aunt" Geneva.

CHAPTER 6

Happy Birthday, Daddy!

Today I am remembering my father. Daddy was only six-ty-seven years old when he died. When I think about the passage of time related to his death, I compare it to my youngest son, who recently celebrated his twenty-first birthday. He was only six months old when his grandfather died. So, Daddy has been gone almost twenty-one years and would be eighty-eight years old today—doesn't seem possible.

I remember I looked at obituaries frequently the first few years after his death wondering who was awarded a few more years than my dad and wondering why—trying to equate fairness and justice to death. Of course, I would see many who left this life sooner than Daddy and knew that wasn't fair either. I wanted to figure it all out; I wanted an explanation. After all, sixty-seven years was far too young to die. Why was his illness leading to death prolonged?

Trying to figure out death is an impossible task—why some depart so young and others live for decades. Why do some very good people have fewer years than some who are ruthless, mean, and nasty? I can't figure this all out, so I will simply remember ...

I remember that picture of you, Daddy, on the beach during World War II—so fit and trim in swimming trunks and a military cap. I remember as a younger man with a family of daughters how tanned and young-looking you were from working outside. I thought you were very handsome. I remember people telling me how much I looked like you (and I don't believe it was simply the brown eyes). I remember that you made us laugh by talking like Donald Duck. How did you do that? I remember that you commanded respect. I remember that you taught by example more than by words. I remember the time you didn't yell at me when I backed the car into the side of the garage. I remember that you were a good provider for your family—that we never missed a meal or lacked a bed to sleep in. I remember that you loved to fish. I remember sharing a love of sports. I remember that you kept all the vehicles running well. I remember the HUGE tomatoes that you grew in your garden after you retired. I remember that you were a man of your word.

You were a good father, Daddy. I only wish that my sons could remember.

Yes, some days I still look at the obituaries and ask the same questions. I still cannot figure it out, but I do have peace, peace in knowing that someday I will understand.

> For now we see only a reflection as in a mirror;
> then we shall see face to face.
> Now I know in part;
> then I shall know fully,
> even as I am fully known.
>
> —I Corinthians 13:12

This was written and posted as a blog in January 2012 honoring my dad on his birthday.

CHAPTER 7

Misunderstood Maggie

Fifty-five years ago today she died, May 4, 1959. She saw yellow—a flower, the sun, or the light of heaven. Four days later, she was buried on a beautiful spring day, a day like today. Flowers galore lined the church as cousin Bub carried her crippled brother Ben up the long flight of stairs to take his seat with the family. My mother, four months pregnant with her third daughter, traveled with other siblings from California to lay her mother to rest.

I don't remember those days—too young, so I am told. But why do I remember other very specific things before that time—events, her mannerisms, her kindness, where she lived—details that should not be present in the memory of a then three-year-old little girl? But I do remember. And I learned other things as I researched family history, studied dates and notes, and listened to stories. I find it interesting that my middle son was born one hundred years after her—1888 and 1988.

She bore the first name of her maternal grandmother, Rhoda. She was called by her middle name—Margaret, Maggie, Mag. She was a beautiful young woman, thick hair and wide blue eyes.

Consent was required by her mother when she married at the tender age of sixteen and was thrust into adulthood on another spring day. Tomorrow is the 110th anniversary of that union.

She was a hard worker and a devoted mother. She gave birth to sixteen children over twenty-nine years. She lost one baby girl and one little boy loved by all. She said, "A piece of you dies when your child dies." She worked in the fields like a man, stopping only to nurse the newest baby and prepare meals for the family. Much of this time, she was also pregnant with the next child.

She was a woman of faith and taught that faith to others, specifically children.

She made a very difficult decision and endured ridicule and criticism by ones who felt worthy to judge. She walked away. She was a strong woman, misunderstood by many who tried to shame her. In the years to come, she held her head high and was respected by all who knew her. She carved out her new life. She continued to work hard. She was loved.

As she turned the page of her seventy-first year, she knew her time was short. Her once vibrant hair now was gray, and her

eyes bore the lines of a life not easy. She returned to her Midwest homeland, a journey that would place her arrival a few weeks away from her eternal home—the thing I grasp to remember but cannot. Instead, I remember the apples, the hula hoop, the coffee with cream and sugar in a china cup, and calling her "Mammy."

I see yellow today, too—the sun, the tulips, and eternal hope until I see the light of heaven that she saw. I loved her.

This was written and posted as a blog in May 2014. More is written about my grandmother, Mag, in *Reflections* and *Helen's Heritage*.

CHAPTER 8

The Two Who Remain

F rom the Obituary of Rhoda Margaret Case—May 4, 1959:

> ... *On May 5, 1904, she was united in marriage to James Bernard Herbert ... to this union 16 children were born ...*

Times were different. Large families were common in rural America. But even in those days, I think Grandma and Grandpa must have produced one of the largest families. Almost thirty years spanned between the oldest and the youngest. My current book project documents some of this family history, which I refer to as "Mother's Story." Today, I pause from that work to honor two of these sixteen children—the two who remain. This month, they both celebrate milestone birthdays, ninety and eighty.

AUNT EUNICE

She tells me stories of learning to cook at an early age and caring for her younger siblings, of Mother sleeping with her and giving her a bottle at night, of marrying young and leaving Mother to be united to her husband, and crying when she left Mother to make a home and life with her husband. I remember what fun Aunt Eunice and Uncle Rube were when they came to visit us in California. They had three children of their own. As a little girl, one thing that stands out in my mind is watching her grab an apron to cover her *Sunday Best* as she finished preparations for dinner after church. She tied the apron in the back without looking—a perfect bow. My eyes followed the tails of the bow down to her calves sporting seamed nylon stockings. Thick black hair, hazel eyes—she was, and still is, beautiful. And we still benefit from her wonderful recipes. She is a woman of faith and has modeled that walk her entire life. She still watches over her baby sister.

MOTHER (HELEN)

Forever and always the baby, she had many sibling mothers. She, too, cried when her Sister Eunice left to begin a life with her new husband. She missed her, missed her, missed her. At least she still had Sister Louise. Mother grew into a talented young woman who could sing and play various stringed instruments without the privilege of structured, formal lessons. I remember one family gathering at Uncle Marve's house in the 1960s. We were on the enclosed back porch with a cement floor and someone handed Mother a guitar. She strummed a few chords until it was tuned to her satisfaction. And then the singing began. Aunt Lizzie and Aunt Delta harmonized to "The Old Rugged Cross" as others joined in. Whatever song came next, Mother swiftly chimed in on the guitar, no sheet music required. Her big sapphire eyes sparkled against her blonde hair.

IN SUMMARY

There is so much more to say … enough for a book.

These two ladies are our family rocks, the two remaining living stones. Wisdom and love abound.

- *Need to hear a story?* They have one.

- *Need to make a pie?* They have the recipe.

- *Need a little discipline?* They can still whip you into shape.

- *Need encouragement to get through the day?* Talk to one of them who has learned what it means to walk by faith, one day at a time, for 170 years combined.

- *Maybe you need a hug.* Their arms are wide and encompassing.

- *Need prayer but don't have the words?* They do and can touch the Master's hand who holds the answer.

Let us not forget the gifts still with us. May we give and receive while we are yet able. One day, the baton will be passed. The choice is ours, but we must make the time. Much love to you both, the two who remain.

"Honor your father and mother"—
which is the first commandment with a promise—
so that it may go well with you and
that you may enjoy long life on the earth.

—Ephesians 6:2-3

This was written and posted as a blog in January 2014 to honor the two matriarchs in my mother's family on their eightieth and ninetieth birthdays. The extended family gathered for a joint birthday party in their hometown. The room was full of family and friends. I was asked to read this blog. It was an honor.

CHAPTER 9

Mother's Day

Don't be confused. You're not reading a six-month-old blog. And, no, it's not May. It is, however, my Mother's day—her birthday. How blessed I am to call her "mother," and how blessed my sisters and I are to still have her counsel, love, and support. As much as she is to us and our children, I am equally touched to see what she means to others—especially nieces, nephews, great nieces and great nephews, as well as friends.

She defines the term "mother." When it came time to draft the dedication page for my book *Reflections*, it was an effortless task. The honor could go to no one else. It was not easy to summarize the vignette entitled "Mother." There was so much to say. At one point, I simply stated: "You have your own story to tell."

Born in 1934, the youngest of a clan of sixteen children whose births spanned an era of thirty years, she and one sister remain the link to our past, our heritage. They hold the keys, the stories of our ancestors, and are still with us and available to share those treasures. We must only ask.

And so, beginning this new year and this day, her birthday, I will make a point to set aside my other projects and will devote my time to helping her tell her story.

Family and friends, 2012 will be the year ... stay tuned for Mother's story.

Only be careful, and watch yourselves closely
so that you do not forget the things your eyes have seen
or let them slip from your heart as long as you live.
Teach them to your children and to their children after them.

—Deuteronomy 4:9

This was written and posted as a blog in January 2012 for my mother's birthday. I had high hopes to finish her book, *Helen's Heritage*, that year. But, alas, it was four years later. I did not give up, although the timeline changed. The concept for compiling all of the material into a readable format did not come as quickly as my first book, *Reflections*. I continued to write and document her stories in faith that the concept would come. Through perseverance and many prayers, the concept finally emerged. *Helen's Heritage* debuted to the world in July of 2016.

CHAPTER 10

The Babysitter's Babysitter's Reflection

I am remembering my cousin Patsy, who passed away unexpectedly a few days ago. Patsy was born a decade before I was born, and I realize that she really wasn't that much older but enough to be my babysitter. As I reflect on her, may I always be reminded to redeem the time we have on this earth.

- I remember when she was babysitter for sisters and me when she was a teenager all those years ago in California.

- I remember that she and my mother had a close relationship.

- I remember that she was a talented dancer during those *American Bandstand* days in the early 1960s. She was smooth and had that gift of natural rhythm.

~ I remember that she taught us to twist and that I attempted to do the mashed potatoes. (I say "attempted" because I couldn't do that dance very well, but she was ever so patient in trying to teach me.) Mama remembered her doing the funky chicken, too.

~ I remember that she was soft-spoken.

~ I don't remember when she left California and moved to Missouri, but when we moved to the Midwest in 1965, there she was!

~ I remember that powder blue, 1965 Mustang—a stick shift—that she drove. (Wow, what a car—and I got to ride in it!)

~ I remember when she became a mother, and then I became the babysitter.

~ I remember how much she loved that baby and that she entrusted the supplemental care to me every now and then.

~ I remember that she remained close with my mother all through the years.

When I grew up, my life took me away from our hometown. I missed a few decades of knowing her intimately.

On the day she left this world, Mother called me early in the morning and asked me to pray as Patsy headed into surgery. I did.

I was shocked when Mother called me in tears with the news later that afternoon and said, "Please let your sisters know." I'm glad my mother was at the hospital with Patsy's immediate family.

Although we don't understand this timing, God was not surprised. He welcomed her home on her appointed day. We are left grieving but not without hope. If Patsy were here right now, I wonder if she would say, "Love today, forgive today—for who knows if you have tomorrow except the One who knew I would not have tomorrow."

In honor of her memory, may we all live, love, laugh, and forgive—not tomorrow, but today.

> Your eyes saw my unformed body;
> all the days ordained for me
> were written in your book
> before one of them came to be.

—Psalm 139:16

This was written and posted as a blog in December 2012 remembering a cousin who passed away suddenly. It was read with much love and feeling at her funeral by a family friend. Patsy encouraged me in my writing and was looking forward to my next book.

CHAPTER 11

The Rooster Bowl

Well, we *are* entering the "bowl" season—correct? So, here's my stroll down memory lane and my rooster-bowl story this Thanksgiving morning.

I woke up early and prepared the normal golf breakfast (another story), cleared the counter, pulled out the recipe book, and stood on my tiptoes to reach for that big old rooster bowl to prepare one of my favorite pumpkin desserts. The medium-sized rooster bowl tumbled down with the large one. Decades earlier the mini-rooster bowl had broken, so said Mother about ten years ago when I asked if I could have the bowls when she was downsizing. The bowls are turquoise and white with etchings of a farm couple, corn stalks, and roosters. But growing up, I noticed only the roosters. And therein lies the reason for the given name, "rooster bowl."

I don't remember life without these bowls—a size for anything and everything. You could mix in them, store in them, and bake in them. A bowl before its time, eons later, you could even microwave in them.

Many cakes were birthed in this big one. You never had to worry about the batter splattering outside of the bowl. I stood alongside and watched Mother mix up the batter and wondered if I would get to lick the beaters or be the "chosen one" to spoon out the remainder of the batter from the big rooster bowl (three sisters, you know).

Mother whipped up mashed potatoes with butter, milk, salt, and pepper in that big rooster bowl—yum the *real deal*, not from a box. The bowl has survived many years of beater clanging and wooden-spoon whippings.

Spaghetti and meatballs were served up family-style in old rooster, enough for our entire girl clan and Daddy. And for you health-conscious readers, that simple salad with the right amount of garlic salt and oil could not be replicated by anyone—so said Aunt Lucille. We both tried but confessed we simply didn't have Mama's touch.

Mama, maybe my sons will have a few memories like I have. Maybe someday one of them will want "rooster bowl," and maybe one of them will remember the wonderful smell of pumpkin in the house and arguing for the right to lick that old bowl.

On this day of thanks, I am grateful for my mother and the memories, and I am thankful for my sons.

This was written and posted as a blog in November 2012.

CHAPTER 12

The Wedding Day

It was a beautiful day in June. When we stepped out of the car, there was a gentle hush in the air. The guests were all inside the small country church; the door was closed. As we made our way toward the steps, the photographer asked us to pause for one last picture before the ceremony.

I had never seen Cheryl so happy throughout the days leading up to her wedding, and this day was no exception. Nothing was hurried, everything was perfectly planned, and she had time to enjoy this memorable day. Yet, as we lowered the veil for the picture, I could see her controlling the tears that so desperately wanted to fall from her blue eyes. She realized in this moment the significance of the day. Before God and man, the exchange of vows was about to take place, and from this moment forward, they would walk together as one.

Now, Erin, this special day has been passed to you. Looking down from heaven, I know Cheryl's desire for you is to experience the same joy and fulfillment that she found in her marriage. From this moment, may you find peace and contentment and, most of all, be blessed.

I wrote this in February 2008 for the daughter of my lifelong friend Cheryl. It's one of my personal favorites. I miss her still.

CHAPTER 13

Throwback Birthday Thursday

*Happy Birthday! So, you and
Mom's birthdays are only a day apart?*

Oh my, how this question threw me into reflection—on none other than Throwback Thursday, my birthday. And, so, I responded.

Well, let me tell you a little story. For years, we thought we shared the same birthday. Then, when we turned sixteen, she needed a copy of her birth certificate to get her driver's license. When it arrived, she discovered she was born a little before midnight instead of after midnight. I still remember her voice on the phone that day when she said, "Now we don't have the same birthday." But to me, we always did.

Cheryl was only forty-eight when she left this life. It seemed unfair, so much living yet to do, so many grandchildren yet to hold. But cancer snatched her away. Today, I'm feeling the passage of a decade a bit—a little tired and weary. The body doesn't bounce back like it did in years gone by. And I think of her in heaven dancing on the streets of gold, singing in the choir, and rejoicing with the other saints and angels. Maybe it wasn't so unfair after all, but it sure seems that way.

And then I thought of a birthday eight years before her death—our fortieth. I had never left my boys overnight until that time when my husband and I spent four days in paradise on the beaches of Cancun. She assured me it would be okay, they'd be okay. I knew they were in good hands with their grandma. But I certainly was ready to get home to them at the end of those four days. So, I flew home in my stars and stripes. As I passed through Customs, the agent smiled and said, "Happy birthday, welcome home." Three very happy boys and one grandma did welcome me home with two birthday cakes.

And where have the years gone?

~ The boys are now twenty-eight, twenty-five, and twenty-three.

~ Cheryl is celebrating her tenth birthday in heaven.

~ Mama recently celebrated her eightieth birthday on earth.

~ And I am still here, too, about to start a new career.

I am thankful for the years. I am thankful for my sons. I am thankful for having known a very best friend for all of those years, that we shared so many things. I am thankful for my mother and three sisters who love and support me. I am thankful for a caring companion to share my life. And I am thankful to be able to work. I am thankful that God sustains us through all things.

Happy Birthday to us, dear friend, one more time—to you up there in the better place and to me below.

One day I will join you, but for now, I will abide.

This was written and posted as a blog in January 2014 remembering Cheryl. The blog was inspired by a question her daughter sent me via a text message (first line of the story).

PART TWO

A Time to Hope and a Time for Faith

CHAPTER 14

Keep the Faith

With a forty-minute drive to work, I didn't have a minute to spare as I swished the mouthwash one quick time and spit in the sink, splattering aqua-colored specks along the edges. A little tad of hand lotion, and I'm out the door. But where's the ring? It wasn't in my jewelry box and hadn't slipped behind the toothbrush cup. I opened the bathroom door in a hurry convinced it was on the edge of my dresser, but it wasn't there, either. I didn't think I could make it through the day without it. I ran down the stairs, shuffling things on the counter, back upstairs, shifting papers and pads on my desk. Okay, this is silly. I'm going to be late for work because I can't find a little silver band with the inscription *Faith*. Well, here goes, no choice but to leave and see if I make it through the day.

You were different. Unlike your older brother's labor, which was induced and barreled in like a freight train with two hours of pushing, yours progressed slowly. Although intense at the end as expected, there were several seconds between to breathe. Three pushes and you were here on the luckiest day of the decade. You turned your head away when you were full, only eating enough to satisfy the nagging discomfort of an empty stomach. You preferred a man's touch and hold—whether your father, uncle, or the usher at church. They said you looked like me.

It seemed surreal—that sub-zero day in January launched a lifetime walk of faith. As we headed to church, I bundled you in your snowsuit that morning because of the extreme temperature, even though the doctor had suggested wrapping you in cotton blankets instead of nylon lining due to your skin rash. In retrospect, I do not believe that was coincidental. The snowsuit had extra padding. After service, the three of us departed through the back basement door and forged against the wind-chill factor toward the car, your three-year-old brother alongside me and you in my arms. Beyond that, I only remember your brother's feet tangled with mine, and we collapsed. You sailed through the air like a shuffled pass to the fullback. Your brother and I were sprawled in the parking lot. My shoes were behind me; you lay in front of me wailing. I thought, "Oh God, let him be okay." But how can he be? I fumbled my four-month-old baby!

Next thing I knew, Gilbert slung the diaper bag on his shoulder, and I recall Patty telling someone, "It was bad," as they helped the three of us back into church. I placed your tiny body on the floor and attempted to untie the hood on the snowsuit. But my hands shook like I had Parkinson's. I could only bury my face in them as they filled with tears. I feared the worst as Patty untied the hood and you bellowed. A small crowd gathered around us, and our pastor stopped and prayed. We saw nothing—no blood, swelling, or discoloration. Sandy drove us to the emergency room. The examination showed no signs of trauma, and a bottle cured the wailing. I sought out two other opinions the following week. I didn't believe you could possibly be injury-free. But nothing was wrong. I needed faith for you and faith for me to live with the consequences of that fall, whatever they might be.

There were no consequences.

You walked early and had your own agenda. You donned a backpack while still in diapers to walk with your brother to the bus stop. You cried when you weren't allowed to climb the steep *steps and find a seat. We walked home, but you never gave up hope. The next morning, you tried again, and again, and again until one day your dream was a reality.*

You became a mentor at the age of two when your younger brother was born. I didn't need to understand the world the two of you created in front of the window where you played for hours. A few years later, he rode on the back of your bike as you pedaled up and down our dead-end street.

A silly mistake on an ordinary day of life left a thumbtack lodged in your esophagus, requiring surgery over a Fourth of July holiday. We rode in an ambulance, unaware at the time of the life-threatening situation. The thumbtack is still preserved in your case containing Christmas ornaments, a letter jacket, trophies, awards, and pictures—yet another moment of faith.

You cried when you were the last one picked for the daily sandlot baseball game—a game comprised of neighborhood boys all older like your brother. I remember when those crocodile tears turned into a moment of joy as you ran into the house and announced to me, "I caught the ball!" You were not about to let the green tennis ball squished firmly in the webbing of the glove roll out. You refused to play organized T-ball. The ball should be pitched, not perched, so you said. Later you joined a kid-pitch team but were frustrated with simply playing instead of winning and finally found your spot on a winning traveling team. You had a hot bat, lightning-fast legs, and a fiery temper when you didn't perform.

You were popular in school with friends, fellow students, and teachers—an overachiever and a good student. You inherited that dreaded burden of perfectionism. By that time, everyone *wanted you on their team.*

You started weightlifting in middle school. You were lean, strong, and small. The gym teacher called you a freak of nature because of your unnatural ability. Your high school weightlifting records still stand. I learned the meaning of "six pack" during these years.

Although your life had been surrounded year round with baseball, your overall athleticism, strength, and speed caught the eyes of the football and wrestling coaches in high school—much to my dismay. I watched the awful collision of bodies and helmets, fearing you were in the mix. One by one, they stood up like pit bulls unpiling from a brawl. One remained on the ground, lifeless. I scanned frantically through the bench, looking for your number but unable to find it. I walked down to the sidelines as a round of applause erupted for the revived player. I saw the back of the jersey—#9. It was you. You insisted that you would return to the game, although you couldn't remember your locker combination or even one of three numbers the trainer repeated to you five minutes earlier. I was furious when the doctor cleared you for play a week later. His faith was stronger than mine.

Even though you had limited experience in wrestling, you lettered your freshman year and contributed on a state-championship team. The sport took its toll on your left knee and jeopardized your senior-year baseball season. You and your coach opted for surgery two weeks before that final season was to begin as you avoided conversations with college baseball coaches. I waited alone in the surgical ward on a rainy Friday night. The surgery was not supposed to take that long. The doctor finally emerged shaking his head. He sighed, "It was much worse than expected. At least it's not cancer, but I've never seen that much infection and funny-looking tissue. He might not play this year."

But you were determined. You devoted yourself to daily therapy and continued to be a senior leader while you recovered. I occupied my mind by working on the baseball yearbook and believed you would play—and you did the last four weeks.

Your senior picture took my breath away. You no longer favored me ... thick black hair, striking eyebrows, and the square jaw ... you were your father's son.

You chose a college path different from what I had hoped for you. I purchased a sweater I called my faith sweater and hoped you would wear the colors of the Blue Jays and play for that coach in Chicago. You had peace with your decision, and eventually I found peace with it as well. I accepted the tattoo between your shoulder blades, especially when I realized Tenga Fé means "have faith" in Spanish. And I considered it meaningful when you returned home after your first successful year of higher education with a husky puppy you had named Faith.

A few days later, you escorted me to a Mother's Day dance. You doubled over in pain at one point, head between your knees, but assured me, "I'm okay. It goes away." A week later, it wouldn't go away. I took you to yet another emergency room on another memorable Friday. What could cause this type of pain? First, they thought it was intussusception, then a colon polyp, and then a benign blockage. Your father, grandmother, aunt, and uncle waited with me this time. The surgeon emerged three hours later and led us into a private room. It was another surreal moment, and the reality of what he said did not penetrate into my understanding until he mentioned "chemo."

I interrupted, "What?"

"Yes, it's cancer. We removed a malignant tumor the size of a baseball from your son's colon." He used the same words the other doctor had used describing the knee surgery—funny looking.

I released a groan from deep within my belly as your grandmother clutched my hand. Those big crocodile tears that once flowed down your cheeks welled in your aunt's wide blue eyes. Your father stared straight ahead without saying a word.

How can this be? What do we do? What do we tell you? What is going to happen to my nineteen-year-old son?

A month later, after detailed analysis of the tumor, several consultations, trips to see specialists, and one final opinion for treatment at a premier cancer center in another state, we settled at home for the remainder of the summer. You acted as though you had recovered from an appendectomy and resumed your fun-filled summer. There would not be any chemo, only monitoring through scans. I wiped away a few more tears as you stood alongside your lifelong friend at his wedding. You returned to school in the fall having never missed a semester and, after I nagged, managed to undergo scans that I scheduled quarterly when you were home on breaks.

It was shortly before that first scan that I purchased the silver band at a jewelry party. It beckoned me in a way I could not ignore. I knew it would only be a symbol, but in my moments of fear, it would remind me to have faith—faith for you and faith for me. I bought two and thought perhaps you would wear one on your pinky. You gently said you weren't much into rings, so I stored it in my jewelry box. A year later, I placed that ring on my finger after giving mine away to a young lady recovering from breast cancer.

Three years passed as though nothing unordinary had happened. The day came to travel for your graduation ceremony. That one day, it didn't matter that we had $80,000 in student loans between the two of us for your education. We celebrated life and your accomplishment—the first college graduate in my family—with an extended-family dinner at your favorite restaurant.

When you returned home, you *called to schedule your quarterly scans. The nurse said the doctor wanted to see you prior to the scans and followed with, "I think he's going to declare you free."*

My faith ring was lost, but I made it through two days. I sat up in bed that second evening to read, propped pillows behind me, and saw something shiny under the edge of my desk drawer. I jumped out of bed, grabbed it like a lost treasure, slid it over my knuckle onto its proper place on my finger, and glanced at those familiar five letters—F A I T H. Then it struck me ... faith was never lost.

A small piece of this story is captured in my book *Reflections* but presented differently in a vignette. I expanded this into a short story as an exercise for my writers' group in 2011. They encouraged me to submit this in a contest to *Ladies Home Journal*, which I did. But it was not a winner, at least not according to their judges. I tucked it away in my file for another day—*Someday I Will Write.*

CHAPTER 15

Barrels of Meaning

Several weeks ago, I was feeling a bit depressed, somewhat sorry for myself, wondering how much longer I could keep up with the pace of life. I had left my young son at the daycare and had begun the sixteen-mile trip to the office. My thoughts kept alternating between guilt over leaving my child in someone else's care, worrying about devoting enough time to my home and husband, and worrying about the many deadlines at work which were on a tight schedule.

As I approached the exit ramp, cars began to stop suddenly and I thought, "Not again—barrels! Couldn't they do this construction some other time besides rush-hour traffic?"

The congestion was more than I could handle on this particular day, so I got out of the exit lane and began to follow a co-worker who had apparently found an alternate route to work. I soon found myself in a residential neighborhood at a busy stoplight. As the light turned and the cars proceeded to go through the intersection, I noticed a man assisting children through the crosswalk. He was smiling and waving so enthusiastically at each car that passed. When I passed through, to my amazement, I was no exception. He looked right at me, waving as though he had known me for years. My first thought was that something terrific must have happened to him that day causing him to be so happy. But the next day when I took the same route, to my amazement again, he was doing the same thing. This time, I was prepared and waved back. Over the next several days, I noticed others were beginning to acknowledge him by waving and some were even honking.

This one man had caused a tremendous chain reaction.

I had to pause and say, "Lord, forgive me. Help me to get my priorities straight, to slow down, and to take one thing at a time. Fill my heart with compassion for others, and when I get off track, put up the barrels again."

My prayer is even though things are not "perfect," somehow my light will shine for Christ and cause a chain reaction, too—if only I could reach out and touch as many people as this man has.

This is one of the few samples of my writing in my younger years before I realized my dream of writing. I wrote this in November 1986. It was printed in my church's weekly newsletter.

CHAPTER 16

To Be a Mother

I went lurking around on Facebook one night when I could
not sleep and saw a comment by someone on a friend's post
... could it be; is it *she*? *She* was thin as a young woman and this
woman is thin, longer hair, and a bit graying. Maybe it is.

I traveled back in time twenty-two years or so. My, how She
rocked that grand piano in our church, what a gift! And She came
to us when we were so needy when our former pianist moved
away. She was a schoolteacher, married, and longed for a child
of her own but had difficulty conceiving. Well, it so happened
that our church had prayed in a few miracle babies, so I thought
She came to the right place.

Several months passed, maybe a year or two ... time does
get away. It was our monthly women's ministry meeting. At the
end, our leader offered a time for individual specific prayer and
asked that She play the piano. Compassion and empathy filled
my heart as I watched her play. My family was complete—three
little boys. She had none. No one at that particular moment was
praying for her. It seemed a bit awkward, but I couldn't ignore
the internal nudge, the impulse. I walked toward the piano and
knelt beside her. I didn't know if She could hear me (remember,

She really rocked the piano). After a couple of minutes, the keys stopped abruptly, and She grabbed my hand. Many tears fell as I continued to pray. I left that evening with overwhelming peace and relief and hoped she felt the same way. I know that many others prayed as well over these months. Nine months later, She delivered a healthy baby boy. Shortly thereafter, She moved away with her husband and newborn baby.

I surmised if this is She, this young man I see in the picture with her on Facebook must be that miracle baby. But, wait, there's a young lady in the picture, too. Did She have another? Was She blessed a second time? I had to take a chance and sent a message asking, "Are you the one?"

And so, as I drifted back to sleep, I pondered motherhood.

They come into our lives, so innocent, so adored. We are so blessed. We do not know what the future holds, but we hope, pray, and believe for a wonderful, full life. We're riding high and really feeling that Proverbs 31 woman who can "laugh at the days to come."

And the days come.

We want everything perfect. We handle everything with kid gloves. Even family members must sterilize to hold this precious one. Wash, wash, wash. We stay up on the latest and greatest trend for caring for our gift from God. They are dependent on us for every single thing. Nothing can go wrong here. Surely if we do our best, it will all work out in the end. Soon we learn that we are not perfect, no matter how hard we try. Accidents happen; life happens.

- *I rested for a moment, leaning against the sofa, and forgot that I hadn't put up the gate. It had been a busy laundry afternoon up and down the stairs. I heard the walker wheels hit the tile and arrived at the bottom of the stairs at the same time as the walker, precious cargo still in the seat.*

- *I thought I was doing the correct thing taking my children to church. I had my five-month old baby bundled in my arms. The three of us scooted to the car after service against a bitter January wind. In a matter of seconds, not understanding exactly what happened, there we were sprawled on the parking lot.*

Most of the time, everything is okay. All is well in the end regardless of our mistakes. But sometimes we are imparted grace to deal with the consequences of our mistakes and our poor choices. We are placed on earth to live out our lives. We have choices to make each day. We learn as we go, even from our mistakes, and pray for wisdom to keep the mistakes to a minimum.

There are so many decisions to make with our new responsibility. Do we adjust our finances and way of life and stay at home full time, or do we return to the workforce? Surely if I devote myself to full-time, around-the-clock motherhood, that will be the best thing. But is it, was it? In later years, we wonder, shoulda, coulda, woulda .... we don't really know. We've prayed and asked for guidance. But then we still have to make decisions. We do the best we can, and grace is there to help us through.

As our precious little ones grow, we guard their hearts as much as we guarded their physical wellbeing the first few delicate years. We protect them from influences that we see as evil. Sometimes, against our better judgment, we have to let go. Sometimes we are right, sometimes we are wrong. There are more choices to make, and we move on.

- *Spank or timeout?*

- *Pre-school? Private, public, or home school?*

- *Competitive sports, recreational, or no sports at all? Do we spend money on dance lessons?*

- *When do we allow them to sleep over with a friend—maybe never?*

We say "yes," and we learn to say "no." And we wonder if we are right. When someone hurts them, it's like they've penetrated a knife straight into our own heart. We cannot separate ourselves from that child. We are one, or so it seems, but not really.

We pray more as they become teenagers. We draw lines and boundaries, and we learn to let go even more—to let them make choices. We have to. That is the natural order of things. We pray for wisdom to know. Who can know the answers? So, we pray and receive more grace. And we live with choices. We rejoice in their accomplishments and are there when they fall.

- What college do we suggest? Maybe it's not the right time. Maybe it never will be.

- What we want may not be what they want. How do we influence? When do we influence?

And one day, that precious baby is grown. Sometimes we receive a call, sometimes not. Will they be home for Christmas? Will we be home for Christmas? No longer can we fix things. Maybe we never could. We still pray, but they may not be aware. We pray that they are making good choices, but it is out of our control. We love them and we pray some more. We hope that they think we were a good mother. We wonder ourselves.

We compare with others whose lives seem to be perfect and wonder where we went wrong, and we see others with even greater difficulties and count our blessings.

We reflect on all the years. There was laughter, there were tears. Most of us made it, a few did not. Who has the right to judge the whys and the hows? Are any of us almighty, all-knowing God? I think not. We did our best and even when we didn't or couldn't, we really were not the one in control. We pointed as best we could, but in the end, they have choices also. And their lives are separate from ours. They are individuals.

We still love; we still pray. But their choices are theirs. They must own them. ("… The child will not share the guilt of the parent, nor will the parent share the guilt of the child …" Ezekiel 18:20).

Somehow, we find peace with it all—the triumphs and the mistakes. We leave the mistakes with the one who can cover them, *the one who can soften, because He is the perfect one, the father of us all. It's hard to imagine that He loves them more than we love them. They must come to know this, too.*

There are those who never had these joys and sorrows. They never had the choices, it was not their choice to be childless, and they do not know why. Some mothers have had to face the unthinkable—the loss of that precious one, the empty arms of the young mother and the empty nest of one lost later. Loss is loss, no matter the age. These are questions without answers. I don't understand but am amazed that somehow His grace truly is sufficient for everything. Somehow, some way, they go on. My heart goes out to the ones who have had to learn this extended grace of God.

Our parental course may not have been perfect, but it's never too late to love, forgive ourselves for those imperfections, and find peace with our journey. And, yes, laugh at the days that have passed.

I awakened a few hours later and checked my messages. Indeed, it was She. And She confirmed that second miracle baby. She told me another story. I smiled at the goodness of God that He granted the desire of her heart—twice. It was so nice to reconnect and remember.

I am sure that She dwelt on Psalm 37:4 much as She waited for an answer. "Take delight in the Lord, and he will give you the desires of your heart."

But on that one particular evening when I was compelled to pray, her story reminds me of Hannah. I reminded God of his word above and that She did that (delighted in the Lord) with her gifted ministry to us.

> In her deep anguish Hannah prayed to the Lord,
> weeping bitterly. ... and the Lord remembered her.
> So in the course of time Hannah became
> pregnant and gave birth to a son.
> She named him Samuel, saying,
> "Because I asked the Lord for him."
>
> —I Samuel 1:10-20

And life continued on …

This was written and posted as a blog in December 2013. It is my most shared post on Facebook and touches my heart every time I read it. This story reminds me that God hears and answers our prayers—from the miracle of conception clear through all of the challenges that might be ahead in our motherhood journey. Another friend had asked me to write a blog on motherhood, which I had been contemplating for a couple of weeks. When this memory was rekindled, I brought various thoughts into retelling the story and hoped some of it was meaningful to my friend requesting the blog. It took on a life of its own that I could not have imagined. I later learned that it resonated in many different ways with several different people.

CHAPTER 17

Resurrection Hope

Winter arrived late this year and has been unyielding to spring. On Wednesday this past week, I—this one who loves the white fluff—wrote to a friend, "Easter in four days, and we still have several inches of snow on the ground. Wonder what those kiddos will do for an Easter egg hunt?"

Well, my kiddos are long grown. I've had my share of memorable Easters going to Grandma's, attending church with family, coloring eggs and then hiding them umpteen times, and sporting those new white shoes. Even if the weather turned out cool and rainy, Easter seemed to solidify that spring really had arrived. So, seeing snow still on the ground two days before Good Friday concerned me—concern for the ones who would have to hide those eggs. And I must admit that I was ready for my beloved snow to leave. A blade of green grass might be enough to spring life into my spirit with hope for renewal.

I wanted to post another blog, but something kept drawing me back to the last one I wrote, "I Can Face Tomorrow." I re-read it and listened to the song repeatedly which resonated in my spirit—life really is worth living, and I can make it. And then, my week was interrupted.

I found myself in the middle of helping a family return home after a tragic accident (no fault of their own) that left one of five children dead and two others injured along with the mother, who was recovering from critical injuries. The small part I played in helping them get home left me humbled, full of sympathy, and melted any hardness in my heart that might have formed over my previous difficult years. I was reminded of those busy days of caring for my three sons, the road trips and trying to make sure everything went smoothly, that they had a good time and were safe. I was reminded how fragile life really is and that sometimes we have to face blows where life is not kind or fair and we simply do not understand. But we have to go on—we have to face tomorrow—and we can.

I felt a little lonely this Easter morning. I missed my sons. They have their own lives. My heart still ached for this new family that crossed my path. I walked out onto the porch and looked over the pond that three days ago was still covered in snow, and there was the most spectacular sun. I hadn't taken time to notice the snow had finally melted. Easter egg hunts would go on, and life would go on.

The sun was so bright and glistened on the water. I was reminded that we do have hope for better days. The sun will rise and shine upon us again. God will give us grace to continue our journey even in those difficult times that we are unable to comprehend. And, as the song reminds us, someday we *will* see those lights of glory—some of us through death and others on that appointed day. Maybe it will be a day like today.

> After he said this, he was taken up before their very eyes,
> and a cloud hid him from their sight. They were looking
> intently up into the sky as he was going, when suddenly two
> men dressed in white stood beside them. "Men of Galilee,"
> they said, "why do you stand here looking into the sky?

This same Jesus, who has been taken from you into heaven, will come back in the same way you have seen him go into heaven."

—Acts 1:9-11

This was written and posted as a blog in March 2013.

CHAPTER 18

I Can Face Tomorrow

It was Easter Sunday 1984. I stood beside Mother as the pastor prepared to dismiss the congregation but first asked us to sing a song. Mother grabbed my hand as we began to sing, and our hands swept against the full skirt of my dress.

I remember the dress. I had made it several weeks before—a spring project to occupy my mind and my time. The base of the fabric was yellow with a soft plaid of other pastels woven into the fabric. The fitted bodice had an inset yoke of a crisp white oxford material—a nice contrast to the delicate print. This same crisp white cuffed the short sleeves. The gathered full skirt fell from the white-belted waist—a very slight waist, as I was at one of my lowest weights ever, 105 pounds. The low weight reflected my emotional health as well. I was depressed and anxious. Would I ever feel good again? How did I get to this point, and what could I possibly do to pull myself out? I was twenty-eight years old, had an established career with a good salary, had been married for eight years, and hoped to start a family. But there I stood not knowing if I could make it through the day, let alone the next week, month, or year.

Why do I remember what I was wearing that day and so many details? Because it was a defining moment, a crossroad—a moment to which I would cling and consistently remember over the years. It was difficult, but I joined in the singing. The words stuck with me as I stepped out of church that day. One step at a time turned into one day at a time, month at a time, year at a time.

Life, indeed, continued on and so did I with a little help from others—a praying mother, a non-judging pastor, and a few friends who pointed me in the direction I already knew—one of faith and hope. A busy life of raising three sons followed the next twenty-five years. Busy is good, life went by fast, and I have many wonderful memories.

Has life been perfect? Absolutely not! Little did I know on that Easter Sunday twenty-nine years ago that I would face the challenges of raising teenagers, that two well-established corporations would leave me after devoting a decade of my life to each, that I would experience divorce after thirty years of marriage, that I would walk through a cancer shock with my athletic nineteen-year-old son, or that I would battle financial disaster in the twilight of my career—to mention a few highlights of my low-lights.

Somehow, I kept walking twenty-nine years ago and am still walking today. I look back to that defining day, not knowing what I would face but somehow believing I could.

My story probably falls somewhere middle of the road when comparing lives—fortunes and misfortunes. You, too, have a story. No matter where you fall along this road of life, if you've hit a bump, I can offer you the same hope I found all those years ago and again today because I know ... life *is* worth living ... one day at a time. Simply keep walking.

This was written and posted as a blog in February 2013.

CHAPTER 19

Vignettes of Faith and Hope

SIMPLE THINGS FOR THE FUTURE

A pleasant memory crossed my mind today that warmed my heart and brought a smile to my face. I like those unexpected feel-good moments, the ones you least expect.

One of my sisters captured a trip we took a few years ago to Lake Tahoe on CD—pictures along with gentle piano music. I hadn't watched it for quite some time. The scenery photos with the music are absolutely mesmerizing, and the personal photos with my sisters, mother, and cousin remind me of the fun "girls" week we enjoyed—climbing the rocks along the water and wondering if we would make it back down, the fabulous view on the gondola ride, the crystal-clear water, the spectacular tree-studded mountains, the bald eagles, and, oh, that music. It seemed fitting she ended the CD with the song "Simple Things."

As I placed the CD back in the case, I noticed she had titled it "Lake Tahoe—2005." Has it really been five years? Although heartache and difficulty have been my companion the past five years, I realized at that moment—wow, I'm still here! Enjoying the simple things has helped me through the difficulty. I may never return to Lake Tahoe, but I can step out and look at the star-studded heavens, feel the warmth of the sun on my head, feel the gentle autumn breeze when I walk through the park, then listen to inspiring music with my family and friends. Today I am experiencing that unexpected, feel-good moment for the future, so I think I will enjoy!

KEEP CLIMBING

When I think about anger, initially I think of an emotion with a bad connotation. I don't believe I experienced this real emotion until I was in my thirties and a mother. Up to that point, I had never felt that sense of boiling begin inside your belly and eventually welling up all the way into your head. Know what I mean? Been there? Surely, this was a bad thing, so I thought.

But was it, or is it always?

Through listening to various teachers and speakers over the years, I have learned that anger isn't all bad. One person said, "Anger can be love's clearest voice." And I have learned in recent years that anger can move mountains. And if they're ones that need to be moved, perhaps this is anger directed appropriately.

I have a very long fuse but have discovered that once that fuse is gone, an explosion awaits on the end. Now, for many people, the explosion I have would be nothing more than annoying. I tend to raise my voice a bit, which gets a little screechy, and to repeat myself as many times as necessary until I feel the individual understands my point. Notice I say "when I feel"—not when they actually do. Well, this is what I did last week. And I don't believe that I moved any mountains, at least not yet. I simply tried to get my point across. So, suppose that my little burst of anger will eventually cause a certain situation or process to change—a mountain—will I then be justified?

For now, bursting into someone's office with others present in an attempt to make my point, barely falling short of uttering a four-letter word—well, perhaps I am still learning to walk with grace. So, I will get up and try again.

> Tremble and do not sin; when you are on your beds,
> search your hearts and be silent.

—Psalm 4:4

REST IN HIM

I received my manuscript back from the editing department of the publishing company early last week after having requested a line-by-line edit primarily to conform to industry standards. I've been struggling with understanding the copyright laws, what's allowed and not allowed, deciding what needs to be edited, and then trying to decide how to cite appropriately. In this process I am definitely aware of the learning curve of writing your first book—you're not finished even when your manuscript is complete. I've researched, gathered information from others with more knowledge than I, and still seem unable to decide what specific modifications to make. I must have looked at my notes for three hours before giving up and going to bed last night. I was at another roadblock.

But then this morning I awakened, grabbed a cup of coffee, and went back to bed—not to sleep but to ponder some more. I turned on some gentle faith music and sat up in bed, looked out my spacious window, sipped my coffee, quieted my mind, and began to pray for my son who was asleep in the next room. He is in town on spring break and had an appointment this morning to have his wisdom teeth extracted. I thought about his life and some of the physical challenges God had brought him through and prayed for God's continued blessing. As I ended my prayer, this amazing peace came over me, my mind was clear, and I unexpectedly had a flash of inspiration regarding these final touches for my book.

I'm still basking in the peace of that quiet moment early this morning and the realization that sometimes I need to let go, stop trying in my own strength, and rest.

> He says, "Be still, and know that I am God;
> I will be exalted among the nations,
> I will be exalted in the earth."

> —Psalm 46:10

KEEP RUNNING

Lyrics, music, and simply words in general inspire me. I never know when this is going to happen, but when it does, I pay attention and contemplate. I don't take lightly what could be God's way of reaching down and encouraging me.

The most recent opportunity I had to "pay attention" was last weekend. I certainly should not have tried to complete that physically challenging task of putting the washcloths in the hamper. Alas, the pain in my lower back took me to my knees. After three days of continuing to work both jobs and barely getting across the street back home from one of them, I went to see my brother-in-law the chiropractor. He made some amazing adjustment, cracking it back in the same way it cracked out, then proceeded to give me strict orders to do nothing for twenty-four hours or so. The twenty-four hours of time happened to be a Sunday with no work scheduled, and a friend happened to have rented the movie *Secretariat*. I took doctor's orders, staying on the couch the entire day starting first with watching an inspirational broadcast and then watching *Secretariat* four times! Typically, I don't watch movies—don't have the time and usually fall asleep, which makes them a waste of time. I could not ignore the message that resounded back at me. This blog could go on forever, and you would most certainly tire of reading. So, I will end with only one encouraging phrase that has now become a part of my dream wall. No—I will not live the rest of my life in regret. "Do everything you can to win and live with it if you can't."

Is your antenna up, or will you have to be brought to your knees like me to pay attention?

GET OUT OF YOUR LUNCHBOX

As I gaze out my window overlooking the park, I realize what a mild autumn it has been. The leaves have been changing for quite some time, we have not had a freeze or even frost, yet the leaves are now sparse. The trees know it is time for change. Perhaps we, too, need a small change—enough to see or try something new.

Last Friday, a co-worker invited me to go across the parking lot of our office building to a church bazaar. At first, I came up with a few reasons why I couldn't go, like not wanting to take much time and needing to buy something quick for lunch since I hadn't brought mine that day. Of course, she had an answer for both. They were serving quick lunches, and I could leave whenever I wanted. Reluctantly I agreed to get out of my box. My first impression as I walked in was "what a bunch of junk." My eye quickly caught sight of these huge decorative fans. Someone told me they were only a dollar and very "retro." Then my eye caught an area of vintage clothing. Holly did her bit of shopping, then came to tell me she had already bought our lunch. I simply needed to come and eat. We sat down at a table full of elderly people working the bazaar. Now mind you, I almost qualify for the senior citizen discount at McDonald's, so you get the picture when I say "elderly." They quickly included us in the conversation, and one funny line led to another. I don't think I've laughed that much at lunch in years. As we got up to leave, I realized we had taken a little longer than normal for lunch that day. But I returned refreshed and probably more productive. And the Frito pie hit the spot.

Do you need to get out of your lunchbox? If so, beware, you might return with five fans and an evening formal from the 1960's, but the laughter will be well worth the trip!

> A happy heart makes the face cheerful,
> but heartache crushes the spirit.

—Proverbs 15:13

THE ENCOURAGER

I have been submerged the past month in finishing my book and would like to refer you to a previous post, "Get Out of Your Lunchbox." I want to point out that this was not my first visit to the church across the parking lot from my office building. A couple of months before that, Holly had asked me to go over to the church, again during lunch, but not for a bazaar. She simply felt led to ask me to go and pray/meditate. I was hesitant to go, similar to the second time she asked—I did not want to take time, and it had been a very difficult day. For some reason, I went with her. She escorted me into the empty sanctuary; we sat down and had a moment of silent, individual prayer. After a few minutes, we both opened our eyes, and she began to encourage me in my writing. She showed me her watch and said she wanted to give it to me because I needed a watch becoming of a writer, a big watch, and I needed to continue with my book project. The events of the day had been overwhelming, and I was not at all encouraged about meeting my goal. Knowing that she loved her watch, I pleaded with her to keep it, insisting that I could not accept the gift. In the end, I succumbed and accepted the watch. On the way out, she picked up a bulletin and handed it to me. I didn't look at it for several days, but when I did, I noticed a very familiar scripture, one that years ago had spoken to my spirit, calling me to a specific work. I was not able to fulfill that calling and have recently wondered if perhaps my writing could be an avenue for fulfilling that calling from years earlier. As I recounted this story to another friend and questioned whether I should keep the watch, it was suggested that perhaps I should keep the watch until my goal was met and then return it. The watch could be my symbol for finishing the project.

Last Thursday, I wrapped up my favorite Christmas gift and presented it to Holly. I bet you can guess what was inside the box. She seemed overwhelmed and at first did not want to accept it until I explained that the symbol had served its purpose. It had kept the flame alive and my goal in sight. I am now compiling the chapters in manuscript format for submission in the contest. Thanks to all of you who have encouraged me in this endeavor. I hope you had a very Merry Christmas.

I can do all this through him who gives me strength.

—Philippians 4:13

THE LIFTER OF MY HEAD

I haven't been able to "get out of my lunchbox" lately and am looking forward to the next unexpected pick-me-up. In the meantime, what does one do? It's too early for the winter blues. After all, the holidays are approaching. Surely, I can look forward to this special time of the year.

I appreciate the people who cross my path with the gift of encouragement. We all need these people in our lives. But what about those dry spells when you are all alone for days or weeks at a time without words of encouragement?

I have found that sometimes I have to encourage myself, don't dwell on the failures, and remember the good things I have done. If I do remember those times that were not so good, I remind myself that today's a new day. Today I will make a conscious effort to do something that lifts me up. Perhaps that's listening to a certain type of music. So maybe I'll go to a concert or buy a new CD. Perhaps I simply need to sit and laugh. How about watching a comedy—even if it's by myself? Or maybe I'll people watch or dogwatch as I walk through the park. The list can go on. I also receive encouragement by looking at where I have been and where I am now or where I hope to be soon. But then sometimes I take a nap or get a good-night's sleep, and surprisingly all things are better the next morning. The sun did rise! And what might be the explanation for this?

> But you, Lord, are a shield around me,
> my glory, the One who lifts my head high.

—Psalm 3:3

HOPE, EVEN WHEN WE DON'T WANT IT

Perhaps you've been able to discern from some of my posts that I have had my share of disappointment in recent years. I don't begin to try to compare my struggles with another's. As I allude to in the post "Be Still My Soul," each of our situations is unique, and we all have our own crosses to bear. In turn, we have our moments of happiness. One day, I was reading Psalm 31. The words in this Psalm uttered my innermost feelings that day, that week, even that year. I had found a companion to my misery—so it appeared. Either I was with King David all those years ago or he's here with me now.

As I was enjoying the company and wallowing in my woes, I read:

Since you are my rock and my fortress ... (verse 3)

No, wait a minute, David, let's commiserate some more. But then he said:

... for you are my refuge. (verse 4)

Now, David, let's get back to the trap set before me. But then he had to go and say:

... but [you] have set my feet in a spacious place. (verse 8)

Well, David, how is this going to work out?

But I trust in you, Lord; ... (verse 14)

David, come on, I sense the pressure you and I both are under—

... save me in your unfailing love. (verse 16)

What about the conspiracy, David?

In the shelter of your presence you hide them ... you keep them safe in your dwelling ... (verse 20), *... for he showed me the wonders of his love ...* (verse 21)

Wait, I'm not sure I want to read this part:

... Yet you heard my cry for mercy when I called to you for help. (verse 22)

Desperately I tried to remain in my misery, but there continued to be hope.

... The Lord preserves those who are true to him ... (verse 23)

Okay—I give up. There *is* hope!

Be strong and take heart, all you who hope in the Lord. (verse 24)

GREAT IS HIS FAITHFULNESS

I'm wearing a little bling today because I feel like celebrating. It's been almost a year since I wrote my very first blog, *Ring of Faith*.

I'm not celebrating the blog so much as the subject matter. In the good times as well as the bad, God is still faithful. So today I will celebrate His faithfulness in the good times. One of my sons is leaving town—returning to college for his last semester. God willing, in December, I will be the one traveling to watch him receive his diploma, his bachelor's, and Faith will no longer be called the college lady but will be settling into a life of young adult doghood (better understood if you read *Reflections*). The prognosis was scary three years ago, but I clung to that thread of faith—the ring—and passed that thread on to someone else. She tells me she, too, is still wearing her ring of faith.

I am grateful for the scores of people who joined in with me three years ago as we prayed for healing and a good report. Today, the report is still good—scans remain clear—and as a result, the prognosis is fabulous. Indeed, great is His faithfulness!

PASSAGE OF TIME

A friend and I were talking the other day about time—how we sometimes plan an event months in advance, look forward to it, and then suddenly, it's here. It really does come to pass. In this case, I had purchased tickets to a holiday concert several months back, received the tickets within a week, and slipped them into a folder in my desk. It seemed eons away. Then, last Sunday afternoon, there we were—living in the moment of something planned for months. What good advice that is—to live in the moment.

I may not always do this, but tomorrow I am going to purpose in my heart to live in the moment. I'm going to shut out every worry and fear for the future. I'm going to forget about the work left at the office (it will wait, or someone else can handle it). And I am *not* going to ponder any regrets or concerns of the past. This one day, I am going to be grateful. This one day, I am going to celebrate. This one day is here, and I will rejoice with my family and friends, for now the time has come.

One of my favorite quotations will be lived out tomorrow. "… and in the fullness of time, it came to pass …"

My son is healthy and is graduating from college.

God was willing and faithful. Look what the Lord has done!

THAT NAME

The past five years, I have had my share of hardship. In the midst of that hardship, I have found hope and peace for each day and a way to enjoy life despite the hardship. But that doesn't mean my world is never shaken. I simply find a way to hold on.

This past week I received some disappointing news. I could have kicked, screamed, cried, and yelled. (I'm not saying I have never done that.) But this time, I felt calm and was mentally trying to assess, process the situation, and form an action plan. The next morning, I was about my morning ritual preparing for work and listening to my favorite piano player on his free internet station. A guest piano artist appeared on his station— instrumental only. Oh, that tune from my past, my heritage, touched my soul and has been my peace since. I'm not a gifted singer, but I had to sing those words out loud with the piano. I was the soloist performing to my own soul. All of the lyrics are priceless, but what grabbed hold of my heart yesterday morning was that my "problem kingdom" *will* pass away, but that name will not ... *Jesus*.

DEBRA'S DIARY: *WORTHY OF PRAISE*

We all have habits—those things we do because we have trained ourselves to do them. Sometimes we don't feel like doing them. But we endure the discomfort and follow through, and in the end we are better for it. Well, I came across an entry in one of my journals today where I see one of those habits. Let me set the stage.

The year was 1995. I had three young sons. I was committed to making sure they had a spiritual foundation. Part of this was consistent church attendance, at least once a week. It wasn't always easy. With a busy week at work and all of those extracurricular activities added in the evenings, it would have been easy to forgo that weekly ritual. I, too, needed encouragement in this area. This one day, I looked beyond the habit. It wasn't about *me*.

I feel so out of place, unworthy, lonely. What's the point in going to church? Perhaps I won't bother to go this Sunday. I don't feel like I belong. The boys don't cooperate sometimes. They seem so uninterested. What a wilderness ... such a war going on inside of me. Absolutely no one understands or can help.

But how can I not go? I will go, if for no other reason, to give honor and praise to Jesus because He is worthy. Regardless of my circumstances, my state of mind/emotions, what others say or don't say, I will direct my attention to Jesus and worship Him. Yes, I must go because He is worthy of my praise. He is deserving of my undivided attention. I will go the house of the Lord.

THE JOURNEY OF MENDING

If you're reading this today, you are still on your earthly journey and so am I. Recently, I have seen so many reminders to enjoy this journey, whatever it may be at the moment, as I head toward that ultimate destination—that place of peace where I can finally rest and enjoy life again. You see, I'm not speaking about my final heavenly destination where I *know* there will be peace. I'm talking about that earthly destination I have conjured up in my own mind. When I get *there*, I will be free. When I get *there*, I will be able to help someone else. When I get *there*, life will be good again. I guess it is sort of like taking time to smell the roses—now!

Earlier this summer, I got to spend a little weekend getaway at one of my all-time-favorite spots—far enough away from my issues to clear my mind. It was a treat. As I relaxed by the pool, I watched as preparations were underway for an outdoor wedding under the gazebo several yards away. I looked at the path the bride would take to reach her destination. Oh, yes, she would have a much longer-than-normal walk down the aisle. But it was strewn with bits of shade along the way. Would she take time to notice? Probably not—naturally, she would have her destination in mind.

I liken myself to that bride. Have I seen the bits of shade along my path like that treat of a relaxing weekend? Did I appreciate spending Mother's Day with my sons and mother? I treasure the day we celebrated college graduation with my son. I am thankful for companionship. I have noticed the rain during drought and the sun during floods—and, yes, I saw the rainbow. I have seen, and am grateful for, the shade.

I have faced many obstacles in recent years, but one overwhelming mountain tops them all. It has paralyzed me in a way in which it seems there is no way out. But I don't believe that. I've been on a long mending journey, and I know there is a way. I see the shade, but it is time to reach that destination.

WHAT DID I SAY? HANG ON TO HOPE!

This morning, I was reminded again to never give up hope. There is always hope, even when we think not. Here's today's story.

My sister gave me a tomato plant around Memorial Day. I don't have room for a garden but decided I would plant it in a pot on the porch with a southern exposure. I watered the plant every morning and every night. The little green plant stabilized and grew and grew. It grew so much that I tied a small stake to the plant to keep it upright. I continued to nurture, and the plant responded well. It thrived even more and required a taller, stronger stake.

I was so excited when I saw the first bloom because I knew that from this bloom a tomato would come forth. I continued my religious watering twice daily hoping to see a little tomato take the place of the bloom. But instead of a tomato, one by one, the blooms fell off the vine. I tried to ignore it at first and thought each one was an isolated case. But after a couple more weeks, I knew my eyes were not deceived. All of the blooms fell in their own time. None of them produced a tomato.

It has been a brutal summer, hot and dry; I don't have a green thumb; and perhaps the pot and soil weren't good enough. I gave up hope, stopped watering, and accepted some home-grown tomatoes from a friend. They were delicious. Two weeks went by and I didn't give a thought to my plant. The drought remained, 100+ degree temps. Another weekend was here, and it seemed the right time to throw the plant into the weed-filled pasture. Yes, the remaining leaves were dry, brown, and shriveled.

But wait a minute, someone called me "Miss Impatient." Looky here, looky here. Do you see what I see? I could hardly believe my eyes. A little green tomato was squished between two brown vines.

I gave up hope, but the plant didn't. This reminds me of one of my favorite books, *Some of My Best Friends Are Trees* by Joanne Marxhausen. This children's book was given to one of my sons as a birthday present over twenty years ago. The boys outgrew it, but I kept it for myself. Over and over again, it has taught me and continues to remind me to hope. No single thing has instilled this within my soul more than this book meant for a child.

The pictures I took of my tomato plant today would fit well in that book because when all looked hopeless, it was not. Indeed, there is still hope.

HOPE DEFERRED

Here I go again talking about HOPE.

It occurred to me this morning that I speak a great deal about hope. If you scroll down my archived blog, you will notice how much. It seems I blog about what *I* need most. I must have hope to hang on in my desperate situation. I know that I am not alone. We each have our own desperate situations at times. Mine happens to be a financial predicament, much of which was not my own doing—but that's another story. This predicament of mine has continued for a few years.

I find myself chipping away at an iceberg that seems insurmountable, but I *am* "chipping" away. The problem is, if I lose focus and stand back to look at the very large picture, I am overwhelmed and hopelessness creeps in. There seems to be no way out. To keep my focus on the daily task of "chipping away," I have to keep the possibility of a "miracle could happen" in place. So, silly or not, here's what I do:

- Buy one lottery ticket a drawing, whichever one is the highest (hey, you never know, and it's only a dollar or two)

- Keep a vision for *Reflections* (hey, it could be the next *Chicken Soup for the Soul* or the next "Songbird"—the song that changed Kenny G's life)

- Imagine that I write the song of the year that Jim Brickman plays and Carrie Underwood sings (hey, it could happen)

- Consider that a billionaire someone would read my blog or my book and want to do something to help (sort of like that long-lost, never-known rich relative dying)

So, you probably notice my tongue-and-cheek phrases. These are my miracle possibilities, and they help me stay focused on the practical thing of "staying the course" and slowly chipping away through daily commitment to my job, my source of income. And someday, like in that famous race, the unexpected tortoise may come out the winner.

You see how important hope is? We cannot lose it. And if we lose it, sometimes we need help to restore it. I lost my hope this week, was overwhelmed, unable to focus, and actually became physically sick from hopelessness. I am not ashamed to say I called my mother for prayer. That very night, I felt the heaviness float away. (Thank you, Mother and Lucy.)

My hope was restored. And, yes, the morning brought about another workday—another day of chipping. But wait a minute, I better check my ticket from last night's drawing—you never know!

We must have hope. Hold on tight to yours.

Hope deferred makes the heart sick,
but a longing fulfilled is a tree of life.

—Proverbs 13:12

THERAPY

Life is a series of ups and downs. Let's repeat that slowly and separately: *ups* and *downs, highs* and *lows, joys* and *sorrows.* Today, I'm thinking about those *downs, lows,* and *sorrows.* How do we get through those times? Given my heritage, the first thing that comes to mind is to pray. And given my love of music, I know that the combination of piano and strings soothes my soul. But after I've prayed and listened, I find that during these times, I must also keep busy—keep my mind off of the problem—do something that so totally consumes me, I don't have time to think about the situation. That's my therapy. I can think of two things that have been therapy for me over the years, both introduced to me by the same dear friend. I wonder if she realizes how much she has helped me. I mention both in my blog "Earthly Treasures."

The first was cross stitching. In my younger years, I cross stitched something for every event. I lost count of the number of Christmas stockings, baby blankets, and framed quotes I made for others and myself. Cross stitching got me through those pressure times of raising a family. This past year, she taught me the popular modern game *Words with Friends* on my iPhone. Yes, my family is raised, but those worries and concerns have simply changed instead of eluded me. I have nights I can't sleep and times I can't figure out my next step. So, I get out of bed and try to remember to pray, but then sometimes I fret. I happen to look at my phone, and guess what? It's my turn! So, I calculate my next move with my dear old friend. At first, she totally annihilated me in our matches. But then I learned the strategy of triple and double words. Now I can hold my own. After several minutes of calculating my next move and finally making it, I realize I'm yawning. And, oh my, I'm not even thinking about that "thing" that awakened me. Let's get back in bed! Yes, I would say today this game is definitely my therapy.

It appears golf is therapy for another friend of mine. He says when he's out on the course, he thinks of nothing else but "the game" and his next shot—all day! After a night of ballroom dancing such as last weekend, I concluded dancing, too, focuses my mind on the moves and the fun activity. Last Friday, I laughed all the way home!

So, there you go. For me, strength comes from prayer and music, but my therapy is, or has been, cross stitching, a word game, and dancing. How about you? Tell me—what is *your* therapy?

FULLY BLOOMED

Have you ever bought a bouquet of roses that never fully opened? Didn't you feel cheated? Roses are so beautiful and yet so delicate and short-lived, even more the reason to be disappointed when they don't completely bloom. Each petal is important to the beauty of the rose, and each petal is missed when it falls. But to never achieve that beauty of full bloom is the greatest loss.

I don't know about you, but I don't want to wonder at life's end if I had fully bloomed. While realizing that life is full of choices—right and wrong, good and bad—I want to have peace that I didn't let too many opportunities slip away. I don't want to get stuck in comfort and contentment so long that I am not open to a new venture. This has not been my pattern for much of my life as I stayed the course in most situations. I didn't want to go to the edge and risk my comfort. After all, contentment is a very good attribute.

But there could come another day of opportunity, and I want to be ready. I don't want to be afraid. For once, I want to take that chance, that risk—or putting it in a more positive light, I want to be ready for that new season. I want to have the courage to step into that next pair of shoes.

Like the bouquet of flowers I set on the table a few days ago, I want to experience full bloom if but only for a season. Remember, life is a vapor. (James 4:14)

Half bloomed or fully bloomed? Sometimes the choice really *is* ours to make.

HOPE AGAIN

It has been a mild winter in the Midwest. And now, even before the first day of spring, we will probably set a record temperature above eighty degrees. I noticed driving to work on Monday that the beautiful dogwoods have emerged—white and pink blossoms lined the streets. Soon the redbuds will do the same. This morning I walked over to my bedroom window and gazed out as the sun was rising. I raised the window a little more to breathe in the fresh air. I looked through the screen and began to *(you guessed it)* reflect! Many changes took place for me this past year—a move, letting go of an extra job that was draining me and yet had become a security blanket, to name a few. Did everything unfold exactly as I had hoped? No, not everything turned out as planned, although I am grateful for the good things.

The beauty of springtime reminds me of the season for rebirth. For those things that did not come to pass, I can hope again. I can try again. When the last leaf fell from the tree last autumn, the tree didn't give up and die. It held onto hope and knew that, come spring, a new bud would emerge and that from that bud a bloom would come forth and another season would come to pass (paraphrased from *Some of My Best Friends are Trees*).

Later today when I arrive home, I think I'll take a few minutes to unwind, gaze through my window again, look at the beautiful green lawn, and remember those hopes and dreams from last year and maybe the year before. Hope can be restored. The season of rebirth has arrived. Simply look out your window!

REMINISCING OF THANKSGIVINGS PAST

When you get to be my age, you have many Thanksgivings to reflect upon. Why is it that I remember one very specifically and it comes to mind every year? I don't know why, but I am intrigued with why this seemingly insignificant one is always at the forefront of my thoughts. I remember the boys were young. It was during the years when I didn't work outside of the home, but I was very busy with running a household of three boys. There was so much to do the day before Thanksgiving, such as cleaning, preparing food ahead of time for the feast, and keeping up with the daily rituals and a few more out-of-the norm tasks since school was not in session. I remember the television being on in the background in a couple of different rooms in the house. A faith-based program that appeared several times throughout the day caught my attention, but I could not sit down and watch because of the busyness of the day. A certain portion of the program was devoted to a series of praise songs—thanks. From my innermost being, I longed to sit down and enjoy … and worship. The songs were compelling … give thanks, be grateful … the words kept resounding in my head and ears all day long. But there was no time to sit and enjoy or participate. My soul longed to praise and give thanks, but other things demanded my attention. Finally, the boys were in bed, desserts were finished, house was clean … I was winding down, too, and the program came on again. I sat down and entered into that quiet place, listened to the words, the beautiful melody, and even sang along, giving thanks to the holy one. I fed my soul—what it had longed for the entire day. It was the very best part of the day and somehow primed me for the official day of thanks. I remember the feeling deep within—a sense of peace and longing fulfilled.

Many more Thanksgivings have come and gone with family and friends, but this one stands out as a symbol and reminder. Tomorrow, when I'm restless and can't seem to pinpoint the reason, perhaps I simply need to feed my soul. Yes, I will give thanks and remember.

As the deer pants for streams of water,
so my soul pants for you, my God.

—Psalm 42:1

SPECTACULAR SALAMANDER SUNRISE

You might have noticed that in my book *Reflections* as well as in many of my blog posts, I frequently use the familiar saying "One Day at a Time." For the past five years, I have lived and walked this way, one day at a time. I couldn't look at the picture five years down the road. I would have never figured it all out. Many of you would shake your heads in wonder if you knew all of my struggles and disappointments. And I am aware that many of you could tell me your tales that would make mine look like a casual walk in the park. I am writing this today because I was once again reminded that each day is a new day, and His mercies are indeed new every spectacular morning. Yes, *spectacular*!

What is my point? Last night I felt hopeless; a certain situation seemed hopeless and never-ending. Unable to sleep, I found myself praying in my closet. Then, a couple of hours later, I stepped into the bedroom where the blinds were raised and right there staring at me through the east window was the most spectacular sun peering up over the horizon. Plus, it was reflecting on the pond—a beautiful hue— and then to my right on my dresser was my first hardbound copy of *Reflections* properly displayed on a stand. I looked back and forth between the two, both reflecting the same shade of salamander—yes, salamander (see Chapter 11 in *Reflections*).

This spectacular salamander sunrise reminded me that His grace is sufficient for this day. The Creator of the Universe, who causes His sun to rise and set each day, will take care of tomorrow—tomorrow. He is able and prepared. The night seemed hopeless, but the sun did rise—and in what spectacular fashion. I think I'll make it another day— one day at a time.

From the rising of the sun to the place where it sets,
the name of the Lord is to be praised.

—Psalm 113:3

PRESS ON

Should I go or not go? It was almost noon by the time I finally decided to make the two-and-a-half-hour drive. I packed an overnight bag, not knowing how long I would stay, loaded it in the backseat, and pulled out onto the interstate. Why not? I had an extra day off over the Labor Day weekend.

It was stormy outside. The winds of change were, and are, blowing ... life, hard decisions to make, choices. How can I be sure? I need peace.

I drove away from the storm. The sun was shining when I arrived. It wasn't necessary to ring the doorbell, but I did. She answered the door smiling and gave me a hug. Three plates were set at the table—an extra one for me. Chicken and green beans were neatly placed on the plate with plenty of other sides all around. We bowed our heads as the other one blessed the food. We ate. I talked. They listened then spoke, each offering advice and comments. Dessert was homemade cookies, and we talked more.

We retreated into the living room and listened to music, beautiful worship music, then talked more, such sweet communion. Then one placed a prayer cloth on my head, anointed me with oil, and they both prayed. I felt peace and decided to head home. I reached to open the car door and noticed my blue suitcase tucked tightly between the front and back seats—no need for it after all.

I placed a CD in the player, pushed the "repeat" button, and listened to a song that I meditated on frequently after 9/11— those uncertain days, months, and years after our nation had been shaken to its core. It's hard to believe it's been twelve years now. This music and these words melted into my soul the entire drive home.

We as a country found a way to press on in 2001, and I, too, can press on today. I will never forget and, at the same time, am encouraged as I listen to the words in this song.

This collection of short vignettes represents some of my first blogs written during 2010-2012 when I felt less was more. I wrote what was on my heart at that moment in time—no embellishment. Speaking hope and faith through these small vignettes kept me going during a very difficult period of time. Encouragement and inspiration are alive all around us pouring out from people, music, lyrics, and written words. Maybe some of these vignettes have instilled hope in you.

CHAPTER 20

Till Death
Do Us Part

Last weekend I attended the wedding of a friend's daughter. I absolutely love weddings and firmly believe in the formality of a ceremony and all of the festivities. There's something about reciting the vows in front of family and friends and sharing your joy with others that solidifies the event. I was so honored to be invited. I don't believe there was a stone left unturned in the preparation of this wedding. My friend coordinated an amazing event for her daughter—down to the last detail, even kissed by Mother Nature. Who would have thought that planning an outdoor wedding (almost a year in advance) in the Midwest on October 30th would yield a day of sunshine, 72 degrees, and no wind! But that's not all—a string quartet playing "Canon in D" on the grounds of a country mansion right before sunset (I think you get the picture).

I can think of two other weddings that stand out in my mind like this one, both several years ago. One was a Christmas wedding. This was my first experience of hearing only strings for the music selection. The music was as captivating as the Christmas tree adorned with wedding lace, tulle, and white lights standing at attention on the platform awaiting the wedding party as the bride's brothers in full military uniform escorted everyone to their seats.

Then there was the wedding of a friend who married somewhat later in life—what a special day for her. It was my hometown church, decent size, and seated to capacity. The bride and groom dismissed each row and, more specifically, greeted each person as they left their seat—what a personal touch.

As I reflect on these weddings, I realize that the couples are still together. While many marriages end in broken vows, they seem to be on the road of *till death do us part*—the way God intended. I'm sure that love, self-sacrifice, and commitment have sustained them. But may I also suggest that perhaps they weighed carefully through prayer and Godly counsel their choice? Taking time to make sure that God is the one bringing you together will make it easier to walk together as one through a lifetime.

This was written and posted as a blog in November 2010.

CHAPTER 21

Dream On

I once had a dream, a plan that would change the course of my life and solve a problem. The plan was coming together quickly and efficiently, so much so that it occurred to me one day I should probably seek God's counsel. So, I prayed, "God, if this is not your will for my life, please close the door because this is moving fast, and I am prepared to forge ahead."

The dream involved drastic changes. The doors to my dream shut as swiftly as they had opened with no explanation. My dream was gone, and I could not ignore the truth that God had probably answered my prayer. I wish, however, that he had explained the "why" to me.

During this period of time, I had shared this plan with a friend. My plan caused her to dream—a plan to change the course of her life and move to Alaska. She asked me if I would help her fulfill her dream and accompany her driving to Alaska from Kansas City because, after all, she needed her car once she arrived. Always up for an adventure, I said sure, thinking it would be months down the road after she sold her condo. Then one day she decided to take action and the "when" became now. She had it all planned—let the realtor continue with advertising and managing the sale of her condo, and she would rent a cottage in Alaska until her condo sold which would clear the way to purchase one in Ketchikan, Alaska. She packed several boxes of personal belongings and shipped them ahead, rented a storage unit in Alaska, and made all the plans for our road trip to fulfill her dream.

So, we set out on her dream-fulfilling adventure—a twenty-eight-hour drive to northern Washington and a two-day ferry ride on to Ketchikan, Alaska. We started out the first leg of the trip with sunshine on a mild autumn day in the Midwest.

We stopped for gas and lunch a couple of times and found ourselves still driving a little after dusk, trying to arrive at our first overnight destination. We were about an hour away in falling rain when I noticed a deer on the passenger side of the road. Before I could alert her, there were three more deer before us in the road. We struck one as they scurried across the interstate. She miraculously kept control of the vehicle even though we immediately knew there was extensive damage because of an awful rubbing noise coming from the tire/wheel area. The driver's side headlight was shining off in the field left of the interstate. She lowered her speed and managed to get to the next exit where we stopped for help. The local sheriff arrived, completed the necessary paperwork, cut away the headlight, and pulled off the body parts scraping the tire.

Lo and behold, we were able to continue our journey in the dark rain and arrived at our first overnight destination exhausted and hungry. Surprisingly, she said the car drove fine. This was a trip that needed to be executed according to plan in order for it to work. We had to catch that ferry in two days, and she had to have her car because she was not returning to the mainland.

The next morning, we continued along the open roads of South Dakota, Wyoming, and Montana. The sun was bright, and the sky was clear, but the wind pulled on the small car, making it very difficult to stay on the road. We later learned there was a severe wind advisory. As we drove through Sturgis, I was sure glad we weren't riding a motorcycle!

Midafternoon we stopped in Billings, Montana and realized it would be very difficult to make our second night destination, Spokane, Washington. We pulled out the atlas and decided Missoula, Montana, was a much more realistic goal, changed our hotel reservations, and kept on truckin'. We still had the benefit of daylight saving time, but somehow darkness seemed to come earlier than planned and we couldn't make our adjusted destination by nightfall. By the time we reached Butte and pulled into Wendy's (one of Cathy's favorites) for the last supper (no Wendy's in Ketchikan), Cathy had relinquished the wheel and I was driving a "stick" for the first time in five years. No one seemed to mind that we drove with our bright lights on to compensate for the lack of a left headlight.

We enjoyed the spacious room at the Courtyard in Missoula and crashed into our comfy beds. Our story caught the interest of the waitress the next morning at breakfast who looked at the car in amazement, thought we were quite the adventurous duo, and snapped a picture of us as we left for the last leg of our road trip. It was another clear day, and the brisk wind continued to howl.

We had received much advice from well-meaning friends and family suggesting we rent a car or change our plans. After all, we weren't sure we could open the hood to check the oil, water, etc. But we came to the conclusion that since the oil had been changed and all fluid levels were checked prior to the trip, we

would simply forge ahead. The airbag hadn't deployed, and we did point out to our concerned loved ones that, indeed, we managed to "fix" the car during a pit stop in a quaint Idaho mountain town.

We crossed over into the state of Washington through the mountain range and thought for sure we were back in Kansas as we endured the four-hour barren drive to Seattle.

Cathy tired and relinquished the wheel to me again about an hour from Seattle. I guess I hadn't done too badly the previous night. I was wide-eyed and bushy tailed and pretended to be Dale Jr. as I drove through another mountain range and into Seattle rush-hour traffic. Oh my!

We stopped for about an hour in Seattle to hold Cathy's great nephews—three-month-old twins—and parted with hugs and homemade pumpkin pie. There was more rain and night driving the last ninety minutes as we headed north to Bellingham where we would board the ferry the next day. Once in Bellingham, we celebrated with dinner in the hotel restaurant. A good night's rest was welcomed as I crashed sideways on the bed after my last bite of pie. The next morning, I left a copy of *Reflections* in the lobby library, and Cathy received a visit from the insurance adjuster who wrote her a check for the "deer" damage. We loaded the suitcases back in the broken carriage that had been our home for three days and drove it onto the ferry at the port of Bellingham. God kissed the sky with a spectacular sun as we stood on deck and awaited departure. After navigating nearly 2000 miles, we were thrilled to leave the driving to the captain for a couple days.

Passengers—that's such a pleasant word. We enjoyed the views along the majestic scenic route.

At 7:00 a.m. on the second morning we docked in Ketchikan and surprisingly were kissed with the sun again for three days as we settled into the Christmas cottage. The views from the cottage were spectacular. I was especially partial to the sunset reflections.

Cathy took care of business, opened a bank account and a post office box, and we deposited things in a storage unit that made it in the deer-stricken carriage. We viewed the condo she hoped to buy. We perused the shopping district and visited with merchants. I chose my token souvenir. It seemed so fitting when the merchant told me they were "dream catcher" earrings.

Then it was time for me to go. I think we were both gripped with sadness. We met when we were in our twenties and had shared moments and memories for over thirty years—years of employment, children, birthdays, anniversaries, recipes, parties, births, death, and divorces. And now in our fifties we would share one more hug and goodbye as I boarded a plane for home.

Three flights later I was home, returned to work, and Cathy settled in alone. And then *Mother Nature* proclaimed her power as an earthquake struck and Cathy found herself in a tsunami warning, forced to evacuate to higher ground. She must have wondered if her dream was going to collapse. A few hours later, she was cleared to return to the cottage with the threat of disaster gone.

And life continues on. She withstood rain, wind, wild animal disaster and natural disaster—an earthquake and the threat of tsunami. But she weathered the storm, endured the journey, reached her destination, and is making her dream of peace and happiness come true. And I believe God watched over us every step of the way.

The moral of this story is two-fold. Above all else, don't give up on your dream. Press on, grab hold of your dream, and do what you can to make it happen. But if your dream suffers a fatal blow (like mine), catch a new one. Maybe it's time to dream a new dream.

Yes, by all means, DREAM ON!

This was written and posted as a blog in November 2012 documenting a road trip full of adventure. It was well received with several comments. What an incredible journey with a close friend.

PART THREE

A Time for Family

CHAPTER 22

Just an Ordinary Day in June

I believe the year was 1999. It was the season of life where everything surrounded youth baseball—competitive, sometimes intense, but always a lot of fun as I juggled three boys in this sport. It was championship Sunday for my middle son in Omaha, Nebraska, three hours away from our home in Kansas City. We had been there since Thursday and thoroughly expected to play in the finals on Sunday, probably three games, being the top-rated team. But as we prepared early that morning to go to the field, my gut told me to pack up everything for the trip home rather than returning to the hotel between games to checkout and load up. I don't know if it was intuition or simply a desire to get back to Kansas City. My youngest son was the bat boy for the team, so he was always with us, but I had missed my oldest son's birthday, who stayed back to play in his own local tournament. I had a divided heart those few days.

I'm not sure why the boys played so poorly. It was an early morning game—7:00 a.m., and these ten-year-olds were known to play better in the evening than early mornings. The heat could have been a factor, too—near 90 degrees as the first game of the day began. Summer had set in early that year. When the last out was made, I rushed my two boys off the field and hit the road in our brown Suburban we came to call the "Subdivision" as the other parents headed back to the hotel to pack. We would be home by noon on that sunny Sunday for a belated birthday celebration with their brother. This was one time I didn't mind losing a ballgame.

I'm not sure it was even 9:00 a.m. when we were soon on the rural stretch of Interstate 29 a bit south of Omaha/Council Bluffs, nothing but rows of corn and soybeans between the scattered exits. The boys were playing with their Game Boys in the back of the Subdivision and didn't notice when we abruptly lost speed. I had the cruise control set and thought it had malfunctioned, so I pressed on the gas pedal, but nothing happened. We were simply coasting, and fortunately we were right at an exit. We got about halfway down the ramp. It was like steering an army tank, but I managed to get off to the side. The vehicle was only two years old, but I soon learned there was absolutely no power— no lights, no air, no power brakes, no power steering, nothing registered on the dash panel. Furthermore, we were locked in with power windows. I panicked for a few seconds, thinking we might suffocate, but then realized I could manually unlock the driver's door. Whew!

From the back of the dead Subdivision one of the boys blurted, "Why did we stop here?"

"Something's wrong with the vehicle," I answered as I picked up the heavy eight-inch (then coveted, now antiquated) cell phone. I called home in hopes of getting some advice about what to do. My fourteen-year-old answered the phone but said his dad was at work.

There's no way we could sit inside that brown beast very long. I jumped out and opened the hood as two older men in a pickup turned off the outer road and headed our direction. They said they were going fishing but wanted to help if they could. One of the men came to the conclusion it must be an alternator problem. They talked between themselves, almost as though I wasn't present, trying to determine how best to help me ... "Nothing's open around here on Sundays ... no hotels nearby, either ... whom can we call ... don't want to call that guy, he'll take advantage of her."

Then they turned to me and said there was a local man at the Bartlett exit I had passed a few miles ago who operated a small repair garage out of his home. Maybe he would help a stranded mom with two young sons on this hot Sunday. He had a tow truck, too.

The two men left to call from one of their homes and returned with the good news. The self-made mechanic was on his way. They waited until the scraggly, gray-haired, bearded man arrived in a rusty, old pickup with an attached trailer bed. "Ma'am, you and the boys are going to have to ride with me in my pickup back to my place so I can look at your vehicle and see if I can help you. Hopefully I can get you back and running today. If not, there are no hotels nearby, so I'll do the best I can."

He hooked the Subdivision to his trailer and asked me and the boys to hop in his pickup cab. I thanked the two fishermen for their assistance as all four of us piled in the single bench seat, both boys sandwiched between us. I thought quickly. If I had to stay stranded for the night in rural Iowa, that was fine. But I needed my boys to be taken care of. I remembered that the other team parents had gone back to the hotel. So, as we headed back north on the outer road, I called up the coach of the team, telling him where I was and what had happened. I asked if he could stop off at the Bartlett exit and take my boys home. Of course, he could.

Whew! At least someone knew where we were. And I made sure the scruffy old man heard every word I said, making eye contact with him as I detailed the precise location. He reassured me that everything would be fine and confirmed my directions to the coach. He must have sensed my uneasiness.

We heard a pop from one of the tires on his trailer as we pulled into his place—a large corner parcel of land with an oversized stand-alone building—his garage—and his mobile home several feet away. There were lots of trees scattered on his property with a beautiful weeping willow shading the front-porch deck of the mobile home. Railroad tracks were nearby across the partially paved gravel road.

The boys played some catch and chased each other around the yard while the man inspected the Subdivision. It did not take him long to determine the problem was, indeed, the alternator. But he said he would have to drive to Council Bluffs and hope the parts store would have one in stock. He said he would be gone at least an hour, maybe two, and asked if I would mind sitting on his front porch as he pointed to a round high-top table with two barstools. He offered us iced tea. I grabbed a book out of the Subdivision and sat at the table while the boys continued to play at least for several minutes. Then they were bored and wanted to get home to their video games and the remainder of their Sunday afternoon. I pointed out all of the different things to do in the country, the sights and sounds, when about that time we were rocked by the sound of a freight train coming through. That definitely got their attention, and it wasn't much longer before the coach pulled up with his family in his mini subdivision. The boys were thrilled and crawled in the back with his boys, and without even a "See ya later, Mom," were headed to their comfort land. I think I heard, "Thank God."

Sitting there alone, I read several chapters in my book and found the breeze and shade somewhat relaxing. There was nothing I could do but rest and wait. Life had paused, my sons were safe, and I was fine. Whew!

The old man returned in good time, replaced the alternator, and had me ready to go in less than two hours. I was amazed when he said I could write him a check. The bill was less than $150. I apologized for the flat tire on his trailer and was very grateful that there would be a late afternoon birthday celebration in Kansas City.

You know what I learned that day? He was not a scruffy old man. He was a kind, gentle man, a real gentleman. I had to trust strangers that day, something I never forgot. I don't know if my sons learned anything on that ordinary day in June, but I did. I was thankful for the two men who first stopped to help. I hope they caught some fish that day. As for the gentleman mechanic, while I paid him for his service, I never felt like that was quite enough.

Two years later, we were back in Omaha again for several days at another baseball tournament. As I checked out of the hotel, I picked up some of their famous warm chocolate chip cookies. The boys and I headed south down Interstate 29 on another ordinary Sunday in June like two years earlier. This time I intentionally exited at Bartlett, Iowa.

Déjà vu. From the back of the Subdivision, "Why are we stopping here?"

"There is something I have to do. It will only take a minute."

The windows were open in the mobile home and I heard a game on the television as I stepped onto the deck porch shaded by the weeping willow tree. I knocked on the door and waited for the bearded old man to answer. I handed him the gift sack of cookies as I reminded him who I was and what he had done two years earlier. He stepped out onto the porch grinning ear to ear and said, "Is it still running for ya?"

"But of course, see for yourself. And I thank you again."

And on just an ordinary day in June twenty years later, I'm still talking about two fishermen and a gentleman mechanic. Maybe it wasn't so ordinary after all.

This was written and posted as a blog in June 2018. It has not yet been picked up by a magazine, but I believe it has good potential. I have received many compliments on this piece.

CHAPTER 23

Hanging Over the Fence

We passed this way twice a day –up and down the hills—early in the morning as we set about our day, me on my way to the office and you on your way to daycare, and again late in the afternoon on our way home. I found peace in this small stretch of road still marked as rural in the midst of two subdivisions—a modest ranch home and a barn flanked by two pastures on either side. Sometimes the horses corralled in the south pasture, and sometimes they romped on the north side. It was the highlight of our going out and our coming home –to see the horses.

From the backseat, safely strapped in, you would announce, "Mommy, I wanna pet the ponies." And if they weren't in the pastures, "No ponies today."

They grazed deep in the pasture—at least a football field length away. And I was always in a hurry rushing to work or rushing home—no time to pet the ponies or anything else. You

*never cried or fussed but simply reminded me at least once a day,
"Mommy, I wanna pet the ponies."*

*One mild autumn day a little before dusk, when we reached
the bottom of the first hill in the south pasture, I saw one horse
with his head hanging over the fence. Before you had a chance
to utter those familiar words, I offered, "Wanna pet the pony?"*

"Yay!"

*I pulled onto the crossroad because there was no off-street
parking, unbuckled and lifted you out of your car seat, and carried you across the street. I managed to hop the ditch in my royal
blue, trumpet-flared wool skirt and matching pumps with you on
my hip. The horse seemed to be in waiting simply for us with his
head still hanging over the barbed-wire fence. I glanced toward
the house across the pasture and saw a gentleman in overalls walk
out onto the front porch.*

"Go ahead," I encouraged. "Pet the pony."

*You sported that familiar crooked smile and said, "Mommy
do it."*

*I reached up and stroked the long bridge down to his nose.
Then you safely followed my example and grinned the widest I
had ever seen. I wished we had an apple to reward the horse for
his hospitality, but all we had to offer were our hands of love and
appreciation. I waved to the gentleman observing from the porch
as we hopped the ditch back to the car.*

This is one of those moments etched in my memory, a stop-
and-smell-the-roses moment in the middle of a jam-packed
life. More than twenty-five years later I *stopped and smelled the
roses* again.

Last weekend, my sisters and I gathered at Mother's to orga-
nize and sort, preparing for a sale. So many things will be gone
soon. Evolution and age are a part of life. The days in this home
are coming to a close. My nephew brought his young family for
a visit. After dinner, we looked out the back door and saw two
horses and a pony in the distant field strolling to the other side
of the pasture.

One of my great nephews cried out, "Ponies, ponies!"

Several exited the patio door with him and sat on the porch. When I walked out a few minutes later, I noticed the setting sun. ... *Déjà vu* ...

I picked up my great nephew and asked, "Wanna pet the ponies?"

I walked over to the fence with him on my hip and showed him how to call for the horses. I had no idea if it would work but made a clicking sound with my tongue and cheek followed by a luring coax. "Come on, baby, here, baby, come here ..." *Chiching, chiching.*

In a few seconds, the tall chestnut one turned in our direction. His mane slung back and forth as his head bobbed up and down. The little boy bubbled over. "He's coming, he's coming!"

The other horses followed his lead. He hung his head over the barbed-wire fence. I stroked the long bridge from his eyes down to his nose as he nibbled at my hand and the now shy lad squirmed in my arms. Someone threw out carrots from the patio door, and I wondered if that was exactly what the beautiful creatures had in mind. The horses extended their stay, and we had such a delightful after-dinner treat.

Yes, some things change, and some things don't. Lines around the eyes reflect a full life. But on the inside, things are still the same.

And life continues on ...

I wrote this blog in June 2014. *Country* magazine published a condensed version of the story and titled it "Stop and Pet the Pony" in their August/September 2015 issue. Several of my readers preferred the blog version (as did I), but I was grateful for the exposure.

CHAPTER 24

Different Times

I t was Good Friday, a mild spring day. The wind whistled in from the partially opened bedroom windows, swishing everything to the floor not weighted down. I didn't mind. This would be one of the few days to enjoy fresh air before we thrust the thermostat into air conditioning mode—one of the disadvantages of the Midwest, hot, humid summers that usually debut a month early.

Days like this remind me of Aunt Lizzie and my childhood long ago. She didn't seem to need air conditioning as the breeze blew in and out of windows in her small country home. The breeze helped dry clothes, sheets, and towels on the clothesline. It was all about family in those days—moms, dads, brothers, sisters, grandmas, grandpas, aunts, uncles, cousins—being with each other and helping each other, very much like the television show, *The Waltons*.

I raised my sons in a world full of modern conveniences—air conditioning, microwave, and a clothes dryer, to name a few—but still cherished family traditions. We stayed home Thanksgiving and Christmas Day for our own family tradition but made time for extended family on the weekend before or after. Every Easter, provided no one was sick, we traveled to my mother's. (My dad passed away way too soon.) We colored and decorated eggs on Saturday (not my favorite thing, but I endured for their sake and their cousins') while a friend styled Grandma's hair for Sunday services.

After church on Sunday, we shared a family dinner, then launched a marathon Easter egg hunt, over and over and over, sunshine or clouds, in Grandma's spacious yard that still displayed a clothesline.

I can't tell you how many times I wanted to hang clothes on a line over the years and watch all my concerns blow away. More than anything, I wanted a close-knit family like I had growing up—like *The Waltons*. I wanted to pass on those special traditions. I wanted my boys to want it, too.

But the world changed—Nintendo, Xbox, boom boxes, and cassettes to CDs and iPods; Game Boys and desktops to laptops to iPads; a telephone in every room to large cell phones, then small cell phones, and then one for every member of the family. I couldn't stop progress and couldn't force the desire for these simple things—family gatherings, listening to the crickets and June bugs, catching lightening bugs, sitting under a shade tree on a summer day when your SUV breaks down in the middle of Iowa, and eating Grandma's chicken and dumplings.

This Easter, they have their own lives. I made the trip to Grandma's without them and without asking. After all, they are grown and live in different cities. I looked for a clothesline along the way. It was a lovely day with redbuds and daffodils in bloom, but I didn't see a clothesline. I enjoyed a few hours with my mother and sisters, didn't have to color Easter eggs, and watched the beautiful sunset on the drive home.

When I shut off the lights that evening to end the day, I didn't hear "Goodnight, John Boy!" Instead, the stillness reminded me of my empty nest. The breeze gently rippled the blinds. But then …

One of my sons called, and I smiled. "Mom, could you please send me your coffee cake recipe?"

Someday I will put up that clothesline to watch my worries blow away, smell the freshness of the sheets from the open air and sunshine, and remember those good old days. And a hundred years from now when I am celebrating in glory, my yet-to-be grandchildren will boast about the best coffee cake in the whole world … the one that Grandma made.

This was written and posted as a blog in April 2014.

CHAPTER 25

Karin's Prize

S oon after I celebrated my eighth birthday, I learned Mother was going to have another baby. I'm not sure it was actually planned, but obviously neither was it prevented. I was the middle of three daughters who loved to pretend, play house, and play with dolls. So, when I learned of another baby, I was all on board to help raise this baby girl myself. Yes, I hoped for another girl even though everyone else seemed to think that a little boy was in order. Daddy needed a son to carry on the family name, so everyone said. I, however, had my own agenda and prayed diligently for that sister.

My prayers prevailed (or possibly simply the natural course of life), and on that beautiful June day in 1964, Karin Joann arrived. As I recall, Aunt Maxine named her and selected the non-traditional spelling, *Karin*. I couldn't wait to go to the hospital and see my baby sister when Daddy came home and told everyone that he thought she looked like me. My other sisters looked more alike with Mama's blue eyes, and I did think it odd that I was the only daughter with brown eyes. I even entertained the thought that maybe I was adopted (didn't matter that Daddy's eyes were dark brown, too). So, hearing this news thrilled me.

I couldn't wait four or five days to see her when they would be released from the hospital and begged Daddy to take me there. But there was one little problem: I wasn't old enough to enter the nursery/maternity ward of the new hospital. Fortunately, Daddy found a way. He parked the car and walked me around the back side cutting through the luscious lawn. Mother's room was located on the ground floor, and her bed was right against the window. She was expecting us and had my new baby in the room with her. She raised Karin as high as possible above her head so I could see for myself and determine if she looked like me. I took Daddy's word for it. I never once heard Daddy say he wished the baby had been a boy.

When they came home, I watched and learned from Mama as fast as I could so that I could hold and feed her. We had a small house that first year of her life. Sometimes I slept in the nursery. One starry night as I was lying in bed and gazing out the window, I carefully planned our fire escape. I would open the window above the bed, throw down as many pillows as I could find onto the ground close together, then grab Karin out of the crib, stand on the bed, lean out the window as far as I could stretch, and gently let her fall from my arms onto the pillows. I would then jump out over her, gather her up, and walk all the way to the street away from the blazing flames. Yep, that would work. Fortunately, I never had to implement that drill—but I was prepared!

I was still carrying her around a year later when we moved to the Midwest with the ever-present threat of a tornado. Mama had been in California for many years where she met and married Daddy but had not forgotten the terrifying roar of a tornado and hiding under a bed for safety as a child. With the move, Daddy had found us a larger house with a full basement, and Mama didn't hesitate to march us down the steps from the comfort of our beds in the middle of the night until the storm passed—even if it might be simply a loud thunderstorm (so said Daddy, who remained in the bed).

But this one particular night, Mama's instincts were on point. The internal entrance into the basement was in the kitchen. As she herded us to that door, the back external door on the other wall blew open and glass shattered onto Mama's arm when she reached to shut it. She hurried us on through the basement door. I was about halfway down the steps with Karin in tow when I lost my footing and ended up on my knees and elbows along with the back of Karin's head on the concrete floor. Oh my gosh. I dropped my baby sister! Her quiet nature was evident even in this—she cried only a little. Mama tended to her, and I don't remember a hospital trip. But that was the longest night of my life. I worried that she might not wake up and was so relieved when I tiptoed into her bedroom the next morning and saw the rise and fall of her rib cage.

We (the four sisters) grew up surrounded by a loving extended family, the two older ones and the two younger ones. The two blue-eyed girls (first and third daughters) looked more like Mama with outgoing personalities, and the baby and I were introverted with more of Daddy's characteristics. At the age of seven, Karin was the flower girl at the oldest sister's wedding a few months after her high school graduation. Even then, Karin's academic excellence began to shine, but she remained humble and quiet.

We grew up with a typical Midwest upbringing and strong family support, but finances were limited. There simply were not funds to attend a four-year university. So, as we each graduated from high school, we made alternative plans. Fortunately, Mama and Daddy modeled a good work ethic and instilled that in all of us. We were able to find our strengths in the workforce and complete enough extended training and specific course work to make it in the business world. But that four-year degree eluded us.

In 1982, we all gathered back in our hometown for high school graduation of the youngest daughter, and I wondered if this academically gifted one would be able to find a way. From the eldest sister to the youngest, the pattern was the same. We each had our God-given gifts and managed to carve out a good life. We married young and provided for our families.

Karin was successful with everything she pursued. She became an award-winning photographer and entrepreneur starting a couple of photography businesses. She also worked in the medical field. She raised two sons, and as the youngest was considering his college options she became restless. She wanted to pursue that one thing her son was about to do. But could she swing it? Sisters and Mother rallied behind her, encouraged her, and she took the brave plunge, making a few life changes.

We watched as she worked full time and went to school full time to pursue her dream. She was determined and persistent and never gave up. There were long nights, endless weeks, and months turning into years of juggling work, classes, and study time. And this week, a little piece of each of us walked with her as she accepted that prize. She is an inspiration. And I want to say to my baby sister, "Your mother and sisters are so proud. I only wish Daddy could have been there, too."

You know what? I don't think for a minute he would have replaced her for a son. I think he would have stood there as proud as Mama with the rest of us and said, "There goes my baby daughter, soon-to-be doctor, Summa Cum Laude."

And I am so grateful that little drop on her head in 1965 didn't mess her up. God is so good!

This was written and posted as a blog in May 2013.

CHAPTER 26

Never Alone

She has compassion and empathy because she alone was there. She remembers.

No one else can understand, no matter how hard they might try, because they simply weren't there.

She remembers juggling motherhood and a career and being torn between the two. When she was at work, she thought about that baby. When with the baby, she worried that something was neglected at work. She longed for peace with both.

She picked him up from the sitter's, drove home, and carried him inside with the diaper bag slung over one shoulder and brief case on the other. She lugged everything into the nursery, laid him on the changing table, dropped the bags, and changed his diaper. Nothing was said, but they were together. She removed her suit jacket, exposing a black and white slick polka dot blouse. As she fastened the diaper, she realized he had grabbed her sleeve and rubbed the fabric between his fingers. The contrast must have appealed to him. There was a slight grin. No one else was present on many evenings—only the two of them, alone.

She fed him and kept him with her in the kitchen as she prepared something to eat and cleaned up the dishes.

He rarely fussed and was relaxed with a bath before bedtime.

She warmed the bottle and headed back to the nursery with him in her arms, his soft skin releasing the gentle smell of baby lotion. Bottle, blanket, and baby in tow, she sat down in the rocker and watched him fade into *never neverland* as she rocked and held the bottle for him—such innocence. No one else was there. The day was done. They slept and, at dawn, began again.

She walked him to the corner on his first day of school. He was so excited, and both were unaware of the bullying he would endure the next few years.

She shared the joys and disappointments of adolescence. She paced when he pitched. No one seemed to notice.

The time came to let him fly. Sometimes he fell. She picked him up and set his feet on solid ground.

As she learned her favorite dance, the waltz, she learned such is life, the rise and the fall, the rise and fall—and learned to accept both.

She went to bed, but sleep eluded her. She sought peace—peace for the night and peace for the next day. She turned on her side as the pillow gathered the tears that no one knew fell.

Morning came, and she found grace to begin again. She realized she was not alone.

> Because of the Lord's great
> love we are not consumed,
> for his compassions never fail.
> They are new every morning;
> great is your faithfulness.

—Lamentations 3:22-23

This was written and posted as a blog in January 2013.

CHAPTER 27

And That's My Daddy!

You've heard about my dad before—in *Reflections,* Chapter 7, and in a few other blogs that I have written for Father's Day. He was a man of his word, a man of few words, loved sports, and died too young in my opinion (sixty-seven). Today, as I was looking for pictures to post on Facebook in honor of him and Father's Day, I scanned this one in and saw so many things that made me reflect and smile.

So, let me tell you a little story.

My mother, like most mothers, took many pictures and also kept pictures of the extended family from years past. I loved looking through the picture boxes as a little girl. To help remember years, places, and even people in the pictures (remember, we have a very large clan), she was careful to write names and dates or ages on the backs of each one. Once I learned to write, I followed her example. So, on the back of this picture, in my own printing, inscribed is "Daddy 38, Debra 5."

That makes me smile.

I'm not sure if I hadn't changed my clothes from church or if it was any ordinary day for a princess.

Daddy was reading the paper and chugging coffee, and Mother said, "Sit up there next to him." He had one leg tucked underneath. I sat that way for many years at the office until my knees got old, and I still chug coffee. *Oh wait, princesses don't chug. They sip.*

Look at the princess's pearls! But what's up with that short pixie cut? Well, the story on that is, according to Mother, my hair became dry, dull, and brittle from having two surgeries close together (anesthesia or something). So, she cut my hair in hopes that it would grow back soft and healthy. The princess had to do a little extra to make up for that short hair ... hence the pearls and dress.

And, yes, let's not forget that dress. Look at the ruffles scrunched up behind my back. I remember that dress like I received it yesterday. It was a special gift from my very special Aunt Maxine, Daddy's sister. She brought it to me one day at home because I had been so sick with those two hospital stays. It was in a *huge* box, gift wrapped with a *huge* bow. I carefully opened it and felt the rows of crunchy ruffles. The base color of the dress was somewhat shiny, oyster-like white, almost iridescent, accented with red felt polka dots and a red ribbon trim. To this day, it remains the best present I have ever received. When I outgrew it, I reluctantly hand-me-downed it to my sister, Kathy.

I see the throw cover on the couch and the inexpensive curtains and remember how hard my dad worked, how well he and Mother saved for his dream—to start his own business someday. And I remember life was good.

My future husband would one day say, "He is the best man I have ever known. I hope I can be half the man that he is."

Thank you, Daddy, for letting us interrupt your Sunday afternoon fifty-three years ago. It still brings a smile to my face today.

This was written and posted as a blog in June 2014.

CHAPTER 28

Let It Snow

Why do I love this white stuff that others detest, even abhor? I don't know. Let us reason together.

The first decade of my life was lived out in my birthplace in southern California. On clear days, I remember peering out the window in our dining room and seeing white-capped mountaintops. They seemed close yet were so very far away, especially the white stuff on the top Mother said was snow. I believed her, although the only snow I had ever seen fall was on Christmas television specials. I remember longing for the white Christmases I saw with Bing Crosby, Dean Martin, Andy Williams, and the like. Snow in these programs added magic to the holidays and the Santa story. But Santa always seemed to make it to our house without the snow and without the chimney. Thank goodness!

I remember going to my older sister's Christmas program at school and loving the part where she walked around with a boy in a winter village while singing "Winter Wonderland" and thinking how neat that was.

I remember one year snow was predicted north of us. Mother planned a day trip to take us and our friends to play in the snow. But tonsillitis struck, and I wound up staying with my friend's mother while she, my sisters, and their friends got to go play in the snow.

The next year, snow had fallen again north of us and Mother tried her best to get me there. But by the time we arrived, it had melted. Was I ever going to get to see and touch real snow?

I also thought it would be wonderful to wear a fur coat, so I frequently pretended that my house robe was a fur coat when I dressed up and played "house." I watched Mother pack to travel back to the Midwest one autumn for her brother's funeral (way too young to die) and was fascinated with a cardigan with a fur-trimmed edging she borrowed from Aunt Louise going into the suitcase. It looked like mink, but I'm sure it was only a good imitation. She told me it could already be cold in Missouri. I wondered if there might even be snow and thought how lucky she was to get to make the trip, although it was a sad time. The first thing I remember asking her when she returned was, "Did you wear the sweater?" (Alas, it wasn't cold enough—she didn't get to wear it.)

Then the year came that Daddy moved us to the Midwest— the summer of 1965—and I couldn't wait for the first snowfall. As I was getting ready for bed on that first Christmas Eve, the weatherman said there could be a flurry or two but nothing to be concerned about. And, certainly, we didn't need to expect a white Christmas. So off to bed I went a little disappointed, but at least the excitement of Christmas was still in my heart, and I was hopeful that the next few months would produce a few snowflakes. And, of course, Santa was still very real, so there were presents to look forward to.

I woke up the next morning, early as usual, and first thought I had slept in. The room seemed especially bright. The house was quiet, and I was sure no one else was awake. Had we all overslept, even Daddy? I peeked through the curtains and couldn't believe my eyes. SNOW! The entire ground was covered. In fact, I couldn't see anything but snow. I couldn't wait to wake up my sisters.

And so, my friends, I learned the weatherman does "miss it" sometimes—a white Christmas indeed. I believe about ten inches were officially recorded and, thus, I finally got my day in the snow with a few more days added on for good measure. Sisters and I built a snowman and had our first snowball fight. And while I didn't have a fur coat, I did have a coat with scarf, mittens, leotards, and boots.

After a few years the novelty wore off, and I realized that snow could also dampen our modern running-to-and-fro lifestyle, but I always appreciated the beauty, especially the beauty of undisturbed snow.

My first trip to the Rocky Mountains surprisingly came in the summertime as a baseball mom. For two straight years, we traveled to Steamboat Springs for a baseball tournament. One of my sons and I thought it would be really cool to return in the wintertime and learn how to ski. We kept that secret to ourselves since the remainder of the family didn't share that sentiment.

A few years later, I visited Lake Tahoe with my sisters and Mother in the fall. Although there wasn't enough snow to learn to ski during that week in November, the majestic mountains capped with snow surrounding the lake provided us with some of the most breathtaking views known to man. And then one winter, I specifically took a winter vacation to Estes Park to be around the snow. By that time, I had given up on learning to ski. It was enough to sit around the fire and admire the views. I still loved snow.

But maybe there's a deeper reason. I love my recently-paid-off car. It's pearl white, the color I wanted when I purchased the car before it. I watched someone drive that car off the lot as I returned to make my down payment. I had to settle for a blue one instead. So, when I shopped for my current car and found it in pearl white, I didn't hesitate. My very first car was also white. I once had someone point out that white is a sign of hope. And I read that white depicts faith, purity, and perfection. *(Hmm ... pondering.)*

Although I do have an appreciation for the ocean and a tropical vacation, if I could pick only one dream vacation, it would be to hunker down with the fire, cocoa, and my journal with a blanket of snow surrounding outside amidst the mountains. Yes, I do love snow. But since I live in Kansas City, I must settle for four or five blankets a year and appreciate the beauty when it arrives—like the other morning. While others were cursing the cold and the commute to work, I smiled and watched the sun rise up over the winter wonderland on this second day of the new year.

I pulled out of the drive in my white hope and, since I hadn't tired of Christmas music, listened to Kenny G serenade "Winter Wonderland."

And one other tidbit that comes to mind:

> ... Though your [my] sins are like scarlet,
> they shall be as white as snow; ...

—Isaiah 1:18

Maybe that's why I love snow.

This was written and posted as a blog in January 2013.

CHAPTER 29

The Cord

Twenty-seven years ago today, I became a mother. I ponder the years. Like most mothers of new mothers, mine told me, "You will never stop being a mother." I have known few greater truths. The physician may have cut the cord that was seen, but no one can cut that which is unseen.

The cord cannot be broken.

Yes, there is a time for every season—a time to nurture, a time to train, a time to instruct, a time to protect.

The cord cannot be broken.

There's a time to step back, a time to let go, a time to love from a distance and watch them run their race.

The cord cannot be broken.

The phone is silent as birthdays and holidays come and go. There may not be flowers on Mother's Day. And when words come, the exchange is unpleasant.

The cord cannot be broken.

As life unfolds, there is a time to rejoice, a time to pray, a time to step back in.

The cord cannot be broken.

For how can one who has brought someone into the world watch without encouraging and restoring if possible?

The cord cannot be broken.

How can one who encourages others to hope not instill that same hope in their own?

The cord cannot be broken.

Mothers must pray for wisdom—whether inexperienced and twenty something or mature and fifty something.

The cord cannot be broken.

Through life's joys and life's sorrows, health and cancer—

The cord cannot be broken.

The most comforting words of all may simply be "this too shall pass" or we can … *laugh at the days to come (Proverbs 31:25).*

The cord cannot be broken.

The cello and piano seem to eloquently express that which I cannot—and I now have peace and hope.

The cord can never be broken.

This was written and posted as a blog in June 2012.

CHAPTER 30

Christmas Traditions

I was reading another blog this week—one that I regularly follow—and, yes, you guessed it—it prompted a reflection. I enjoy reading her blog because she reminds me of "me" twenty years ago. So, here is my reflection inspired by someone else's blog.

One of my Christmas traditions when raising my boys was to select a special family Christmas card. Great care and consideration were placed into selecting the perfect card each year that would be sent to over one hundred family members and friends. I wanted it to have meaning and to touch people's hearts. I would include the typical family letter updating everyone on the boys' progress for the year along with the very standard school photos. Then, after addressing all of the envelopes, I would keep one copy of that card, date it, and turn it into an ornament for our very large Christmas tree. I remember many of the cards, but one stands out as my all-time favorite.

Christmas, as we know, can be stressful, especially when raising children. You want to give them their hearts' desires and sometimes overextend financially. You want to buy that special gift for your spouse or parents and sometimes fear that it may not be what they would have selected. The preparations for that one special day: shopping, baking, cooking, organizing family gatherings along with attending school programs, office parties, and church programs … such a busy time.

The card I am remembering put everything into perspective that year. The scene on the front of the card was a modest one—a cozy fire glowing in the small fireplace, a rocking chair to the side. It was *not* an elaborate room. A little boy was standing facing the fireplace with a teddy bear dragging the floor from the fingertips of his right hand. You couldn't see his face—only the backside of his hair and pajamas. He was peering up to the mantle where a nativity was displayed. He seemed to want to see it all, standing on his tiptoes on the braided rug to get a better view. It was not a photograph but rather an artist's rendering of a somewhat dated era. The inside of the card read:

When you get right down to it, the only thing that really matters is Jesus.

This was indeed the perfect card, not only for that year but for every year. I remember receiving more comments than usual on the card. The words in this card are timeless, evident in that I found the same words in a card for sale this Christmas—twenty years later. The front design was different but still involved a nativity scene.

I am reminded of another tradition when I walk into my living room and see the nativity set belonging to my grandmother. Growing up, I didn't realize it had been hers. My mother displayed it every Christmas in our living room. I never questioned its origin throughout the years. It simply always "was." Then one year as a young woman in my twenties, I asked my mother what she had done with the nativity set. She responded, "You mean, my mother's?"

The nativity pieces were in a box in the garage, but the stable had deteriorated and had been thrown away a few years earlier. She then told me the "story." She had purchased it for her mother over forty years ago as a teenager because her mother was a little depressed that year and wasn't going to decorate for Christmas. So, the tradition of the nativity began with this gift from my mother to my grandmother. Even though Mammy (Grandmother) died a few years after that, my mother displayed it every year in her own living room.

I humbly asked, "May I have the pieces?" She gave them to me, and I purchased a stable at a crafts store. Like my mother, I displayed it every Christmas in my living room or dining room. The boys grew up with it like I had—it always "was." Now they can know the story—the tradition.

Although the boys are grown and the tradition of selecting the family card is a thing of the past, the words in that very special card ring true. Now I worry about finances—college expenses. I worry about their choices and mine. I try to work in all the activities at the office, stay in touch with family and friends through various social media, and, oh, maybe I should try to work in that Christmas Eve service, too. I still wear my "ugly" Christmas sweater that's not so ugly to me and the earrings my youngest son gave me for Christmas about fifteen years ago—hooks with small red and green beads and a Santa dangling at the bottom.

You know, maybe it's time for some new traditions. But this one thing I know as I look at my grandmother's nativity:

The only thing that really matters is Jesus.

This was written and posted as a blog in December 2011.

CHAPTER 31

Once a Bridesmaid

Once before the age of twenty, I was a maid of honor. And once before that, I was a bridesmaid—what an honor, especially since, unbeknownst to me, I would never have a formal ceremony of my own. I was only fifteen. My blonde hair, straight but full of body, gently draped down the middle of my back, touching the satin peacock-blue gown. The princess inside of me was thrilled that the bride chose formal-length gowns for us—and, oh, those silver shoes. Following the ceremony, I was escorted on the arm of Prince Charming—the groom's tall, handsome uncle.

Enough about me—what about the bride? She wore a borrowed dress, simple but lovely. I remember her sewing a lace trim around the train and adding some sequins to the veil. The A-line skirt was perfect for her petite frame. She had been my lifelong mentor—herself, still a teenager—my eldest sister.

Through the years, she taught me how to play jacks, hopscotch, and tetherball. She taught me to read music, play the accordion, sew, bowl, and twirl a baton. Before teaching me to drive, she drove me *everywhere*… church, school, work, and parties. Following this special ceremony, on the 26th day of November 1971, things would change. I would move into her larger bedroom and would soon be driving myself. We no longer lived together, but we were still sisters. The groom became the brother I never had—protector, advisor, and helper.

They started their family within a couple years of their young marriage and were blessed with two healthy sons. Today, those sons are grown, the two of them are grandparents, and we ask, "Where did the years go?" Sister is still mentoring, encouraging, advising, organizing; is successful in the corporate world; and we call her *the boss*.

It seems like only yesterday we were listening to the song "We've Only Just Begun" in honor of the formal exchange of vows (what a perfect song). Like all of us, they experienced a few disappointments along the way. But their marriage has stood the test of time. I have to say that theirs is among my hall of fame weddings, and I am so blessed to have them in my life.

Congratulations on your fortieth wedding anniversary. Wow!

> For this reason a man will leave
> his father and mother
> and be united to his wife,
> and the two will become one flesh.
> So they are no longer two, but one flesh.

—Mark 10:7-8

This was written and posted as a blog in November 2011.

CHAPTER 32

And It Came to Pass

There's nothing like Christmastime for a child to learn patience. There's so much anticipation, hype, and expectation leading up to this day. And then finally the day is here and gone. Or, in other words, the culmination is: *and it came to pass.*

Much hope abounds in these five little words—*and it came to pass.* Reading these words in stories or seeing things *come to pass* in others' lives gives us hope for our own circumstances.

These words are used repeatedly in the Christmas story told in the gospel of Luke (King James Version). *And it came to pass ... and it came to pass ... and it came to pass.* Everything came to pass as prophesied and in the fullness of time.

I remember a time in my life when I was discouraged. I was a mother of two little boys but wanted to complete my family with a third child, and I felt like I was under a time crunch. I miscarried a baby, and many people thought that since I had two children, this little misfortune would quickly fade away. They were wrong. My husband and I both were surprised with the grief that consumed me.

Why had this happened? Was God angry with me? I knew many others had suffered the same loss and more. But when

133

acquaintances tried to console me with similar words like these, well, those words were anything but consoling. Of course, others had suffered more than I. And, of course, I was grateful for my two healthy sons whom I loved with my whole heart. But I still ached and suffered loss.

I thrust myself into Gods love book of Psalms to remind myself that He did care and love me. Each time that I came across a promise or statement of His love or concern, I highlighted it and re-read it. And I re-read stories like the Christmas story and soaked in the words ... *and it came to pass ... and it came to pass ... and it came to pass.*

And it came to pass that my hope was restored. Faith arose again. I was bold and declared, "I will have another child, a Christmas child."

Well, maybe some thought I was really going out on a limb by saying that, but we all need a little miracle every now and then. *And it came to pass* like He impressed upon me and I declared. At Christmas time the following year, my third son was born.

Oh, I realize that some would question my use of the word "miracle" here. But, you see, for me, I needed to believe again, to hope again. He was my miracle of hope.

Whenever I reflect on this season of the Lord's birth, I reflect on my personal miracle when He heard my cry and granted my wish. *And it came to pass.*

Twenty-two birthdays have now passed, and I still need to be reminded ... *and it came to pass ... and it came to pass.* Today's needs and desires are different, but remembering yesterday's miracle gives me strength to abide while I wait.

I will abide and hope today, tomorrow, next week, next month, and the next if necessary. Maybe this will be the year that I will once again say... *and it came to pass.*

This was written and posted as a blog in December 2012.

CHAPTER 33

Humbled

For the past several years, I have made a conscious effort not to pass judgment on others or to think more highly of myself (in most cases). However, this week, I learned a new lesson in humility. One thing I haven't had much tolerance or understanding for is people consistently losing or causing damage to their cell phones. I raised three sons who had their share of challenges when it came to these mobile devices. They all had more sophisticated devices than I and seemed to routinely need replacements. You name it, they did it with their cell phones—smashed them, ran over them, had them in their pockets when they went swimming, launched them when angry, snapped them in half on accident and on purpose, left them at friends' homes and would never recover them, even run over them in the track of the car seat. Yes, I got to a point where I said, this is stupidity, and I will not purchase any more (but I did). My grown male co-workers were no better—story after story of needing a new Blackberry. I was so proud that somehow my simple little cell phone would last for years, and I didn't see the need to purchase anything new until absolutely necessary. When I did, it would be one of the least expensive phones on the market.

Well, about a year ago, I splurged on myself and bought an iPhone when my very adequate flip phone stopped flipping. I think it was four years old. I only bought the iPhone when I learned that I had been paying for a data plan that I wasn't using. One year later, I'm still not sure that I know how to use all of the features, but I have found it to be pretty cool to have all things at my fingertips—calling, texting, email, weather, etc. I bought a cover for extra protection in the unlikely event that I might drop it and thought this should last me about five years.

So, what did I do one year after purchasing it?

Dropped it in my coffee.

Yes, you heard me correct—dropped it in my coffee! My hands were full of papers and folders, but the person standing next to me grabbed it and quickly dried it off. I called one of my sons and fessed up. Rather surprised, he advised me to put it in a baggy with rice. Well, the verdict's still out as to whether it survived, but one thing I know for sure: I will never, never say or think that "I would never do that."

Dropped it in my coffee? I was, and am, humbled.

> Pride goes before destruction,
> a haughty spirit before a fall.
>
> —Proverbs 16:18

This was written and posted as a blog in April 2011.

PART FOUR

A Time to Let Go

CHAPTER 34

Of Flags and Regret

Oh, to have the wisdom of "fifty something"
when we are but only nineteen.

It was 4:15 p.m. and had been a slow day that I was anxious to see end. I shifted things on my desk and stacked folders to be audited in the morning on the left corner when the telephone rang. It was Captain Reynolds.

"Specialist, you need to report to Main Post Headquarters in the morning at 7:30."

One thing you learn in the military is to never question your commanding officer. "Yes sir. I'll be there."

"Someone from West Point wants to talk with you. Go to room 234."

It wasn't the first time I had been called to an out-of-the-ordinary meeting. The last time I was asked if I would pose for a joint military recruitment poster. I agreed but never heard from them again, so I wondered what this meeting could be about.

The next morning, I arrived fifteen minutes early in combat fatigues—strange attire for a finance job in a regular office setting but was quite appropriate for the First Infantry Division. It was a crisp October morning, and I was glad I had remembered to wear my field jacket. I stopped to remove an orange maple leaf stuck in the lace of my boot as I opened the door into Headquarters and headed up the stairs. I slipped through the open door of office 234 and saw a fortyish-looking man with a thick black moustache and silver colonel insignia on his collar flipping through a folder. He looked up and said, "Specialist, Colonel Smith here. Please have a seat. I need to ask you a few questions."

He was matter of fact, yet polite. "Why did you join the Army?"

I was certain he didn't want to be thrust into all the details. I came from a very simple life in a small town where finances were limited and less than a quarter of the girls attended college. The majority got married or found jobs. I was a good student, however, and intended to attend a four-year university after graduation. My well-meaning intention lacked appropriate knowledge and planning. I hadn't a clue on the process required to apply, be accepted, and attend a formal university. Somehow, I fell through the cracks when it came to receiving guidance for this process during my high school years, which angered a very supportive business teacher when she learned of my alternative plan. I squashed an engagement with my high school sweetheart as I entered my senior year and yearned for something different—a taste of the real world. I didn't want to be trapped in the cocoon of small-town philosophy. So, I shocked my family and friends and joined the military. It was a far cry from dresses, matching shoes, baton twirling, ice skates, and a lifelong dream of dancing. Joining the military in the mid-seventies appealed to me because I could use the GI Bill to fund my education a few years later. I scored high on the entrance exam and was allowed to attend advanced training in any field desired except auto mechanics. After basic training and extended training in finance, I was assigned to a regular position where I worked and interacted with civilians even though I was in the Army. I enjoyed military life and my work and enrolled in night courses at a nearby state university. I coasted according to plan until I met that one man.

I spared the colonel and modestly answered, "To travel and receive educational benefits."

"Well, at this pace, it's going to take you a decade to finish your degree. We have another way in mind."

I felt like he had a video play-by-play of my life as he prodded with various questions. What was the meaning of this? About a half hour into the session, I realized I was being interviewed to be in the first graduating class at West Point to include female cadets. At the end of the session, he said I was an acceptable candidate.

He concluded, "You are the only person on this post being interviewed, and we are taking only four or five in total. We feel it is best to do a trial run with women who are already exposed to military life. Much planning and orientation is required prior to the next session. I am sorry, but you have only two weeks to confirm the appointment."

This should have been a *no brainer*. But at nineteen, the eight-year commitment seemed an eternity. To add to my confusion, that one man returned to town and had no desire to be held captive by military life. At the beginning of the summer, I left for a two-week leave in June to attend my best friend's wedding in the neighboring state, Missouri. He left at the same time for New York to visit his family. I returned as scheduled after the wedding and waited for his call ... and waited and waited. Long before the day of cell phones, there was no way to reach out to him. I only knew his name, had never met his parents, and my attempts at finding a phone number for them failed. I was emotionally exhausted and filled my spare time with designing and sewing a wedding gown for a ceremony we had planned in the coming winter—a gown that was never worn. I crafted several scenarios in my mind of what might have happened to him but ultimately accepted that I had been dumped. It had been a long depressing summer.

I resolved not to accept the appointment. Quite frankly, I didn't realize the opportunity that I let slip away until years later. This was a once-in-a-lifetime chance that would not come again. I was in love and chose my heart over my head.

I set my course with this decision and lived the traditional family life. It was not a bad choice. I married that one man two months later at the local courthouse, and I left the military the following year. My shoes changed from combat boots to high heels in the corporate world. Ten years passed, and we were blessed with a healthy baby boy. Within five years, another two sons completed our family. I donned sneakers, left my corporate career, and celebrated life with bottles, diapers, Disney movies, and a treasured minivan.

But six years later, I sobbed and was rattled with fear when I realized I would have to return to the business world. Holy cow, corporate life had changed from *Selectric* typewriters and mainframe systems to a personal computer on every desk! I had to start all over from scratch—at the bottom. It occurred to me that by the time our first son was born, I would have been well beyond the eight-year West Point commitment, and I had already had a successful business career. I dried my tears as I exchanged sneakers for high heels once again. A year later, I was in full swing switching between high heels in the daytime and baseball cleats at night and on the weekends as I juggled the roles of wife, career woman, mom, and baseball manager. It was a life overflowed with much joy.

Then one day I faced the empty nest and a divorce all at one time. I pondered life's decisions: past, present, and future, and reflected on not achieving my potential in that very first career. I lived for the moment rather than the future, and maybe that *is* and *was* the better road. I appreciated the blessings of a family life but perhaps could have had both.

Last Memorial Day I embarked on a day's journey to attend a family reunion in my small hometown. This memory of a lost opportunity smacked me in the face as I circled the on-ramp to the interstate. Right there, in the wide-open plain twice the size of a football field, a sea of American flags was planted into the ground—more flags than one could count—rows and rows of old glory blowing out in full honor standing at attention. Patriotism and pride rose from within my soul as I remembered. And it struck me: I might have worked in the Pentagon and White House or retired a general by now. I should have tried for it all.

I composed this story several different ways for different things and at one point in 2011 submitted this version as a short story contest entry for the magazine *Real Simple*. I also posted a blog version without the dialogue in November 2011 for Veteran's Day and titled it "One Thing I Regret" when I learned it was not selected as the winner for the contest. Although it did not win, I enjoy re-reading this story. It reminds me that we all have opportunities and choices in life, and sometimes there is fate, luck, and destiny. In the end, the most important thing is to find peace with it all.

CHAPTER 35

In Loving Memory of Sean Bradley

He was a true miracle child
Such a precious little gift,
Who came to us in summer
Oh—what an uplift!

Though his life was short
He brought so much,
… love, joy, unity
And his own little touch.

Our sorrow is so great
It's hard to continue on,
But God has promised inner healing
If him we lean upon.

As the years go by and by
The burden will be lighter,
His memory will always linger
But the days will be brighter.

And when our journey on earth is through
And we are never more to roam,
We know that we shall see him
For Sean has gone home.

I wrote this poem for a friend and coworker in May of 1987. The sudden loss of her nine-month-old son was devastating to all of us who were in our childbearing years and knew her. We wanted to take away her pain and hung tight to our own babies. I remembered a poem that appeared in one of my high school yearbooks about my sister's classmate who was tragically killed in a car crash at the age of fifteen. The poem brought such peace to me when I read it. I wanted my friend to somehow find that peace, so I looked high and low for the book to share the poem with her, to no avail. I could only remember the last line of the poem, "for Patty has gone home." Hence, I wrote this poem about baby Sean and used that last line of the poem in my yearbook for the ending to this poem. Over the years, I hope it brought peace to my friend who had to endure the thing I imagined would be my worst nightmare.

CHAPTER 36

Family Ties

As a little girl for as far back as I can remember, I loved looking at our family photos. Some of them were in small paper albums, some were protected in envelopes, and all were stored in a large box. I could spend hours looking at years past seeing relatives I knew as well as many I had never met. We lived in southern California, but half of our family on both sides was in

Missouri. One of my very favorite pictures was a black-and-white, glossy wedding photo in a large manila envelope. Oh, that dress ... it stirred the princess inside of me. I imagined someday I would wear a dress like that. It was the most beautiful dress I had ever seen, and the bride wore it well. She was tiny and beautiful, too. Mama told me the groom was my cousin—Daddy's nephew—and that someday I would get to meet them—Dale and Linda.

The first time that I remember meeting them was the summer of 1962 when we visited family in Missouri. By that time, they had two little boys. My grandpa (Daddy's dad) raised Shetland ponies and loved to let his grandchildren and great-grandchildren ride these little guys. We loved it—well, most of us did. I love this picture of my Aunt Fran trying to convince her grandsons this was a fun thing to do. She was laughing; they seemed terrified.

We moved from California to the Midwest in 1965 and visited family more often even though we weren't all living in the same town. Although we eventually moved closer to my mother's family, we managed to see my dad's family a couple of times a year. Thanksgiving lunch was a tradition with Daddy's family. Even after rural life with the ponies ended as Grandpa and Grandma aged and moved into the nearby town, we still made the two-hour trip every Thanksgiving morning to Grandma and Grandpa's.

My paternal grandpa died in 1974, but Grandma still insisted on hosting Thanksgiving even though she was nearly blind. I remember that Linda was such a practical person and was concerned that this was too much work for our aging grandma.

Everyone was getting older, growing up, and moving on with their individual lives. When Aunt Maxine traveled from California for a visit in 1981, Grandma wanted us all to gather again. I was busy in Kansas City with work and my life and decided it simply was not going to work for me to make the three-hour drive that day. So, early that morning I called to tell her. I can hear her voice as clearly today as I did then in her Midwestern drawl. "Debbie, are you comin'?"

"No, I'm sorry. I can't make it. Please tell everyone hello for me."

I wish I had made the time.

The following year, on a cold day in January of 1982, Grandma died. We all gathered again—one final time in Grandma's home. There have been a few reunions over the past thirty years—not enough, but we're still family.

Earlier this month, we received news that Linda had passed away. Sister Vickie and I traveled south a couple of hours for the funeral and wondered what other family members might be there. It so happened that the day of her funeral would have been my dad's ninety-third birthday, but he had been gone over twenty-five years. I remembered that Linda and Dale were at the hospital when Daddy died. Vickie and I talked as we traveled about how life might have been different had he not died at the age of sixty-seven. What if he had lived another twenty years? All of our lives would be, at the least, a little different. It seems like only yesterday we were living in California.

But here we were in 2017 on another cold January day, saying goodbye to another family member, and we understand how fleeting life is—a breath one day and a breath the next—then it's gone. Tick, tick, tick.

It was good to see family members we had not seen for a while—an uncle, an aunt, and five cousins, among many others.

Those closest to Linda lost a wife, mother, and grandmother. I am so sorry for this loss—an earthly loss that is sometimes hard for us to comprehend as a heavenly gain.

And so, we are told to "occupy." But as I "occupy," I also choose to remember. Tick, tick, tick.

Someday all of us will understand this completely—rest in peace.

This was written and posted as a blog in January 2017.

CHAPTER 37

Reflection on Life

A couple of months ago, life, God, the universe, or maybe fate threw up a stop sign, and life changed. During this pause, I have cried, prayed, and pondered. That other word that has become a core word the past seven years as a writer has been pronounced even more—*reflection.* I have reflected on my entire life. I have relived moments in time, reheard and rehearsed words spoken many years ago, looked at pictures of years gone by, and reread journal entries of long ago. One entry grabbed my attention. I was not the author. I had read another author's meditation, and on January 1, 2000—the beginning of a new year, a new decade, a new century, and a new millennium—I wrote her words in my journal on this historic new day. She said that fate keeps happening, that we have options along the way, and that we have the ability to alter our present and our future (paraphrased from *Meditations for Women Who Do Too Much*).

Now, for a person of faith, I really have to ponder these words because I believe in an all-powerful, all-knowing God who sets everything in place. And yet He gave us free will. I thought about how many times since the year 2000 I changed my course, which altered my future—switched jobs twice, walked through a divorce, moved twice, to name a few. Sometimes drastic things happened that forced my decision. And so recently, that was the case again—my life and those of ones closest to me changed forever in July 2017. Fate happened, and now there are new and different choices again. I want to make the correct choices for me and the ones I love.

In the middle of my self-absorption over the past couple of months, I received an unexpected message from a stranger, another author, who had come across my publication in *Country Extra* magazine, "Handwritten Treasures." The author then followed up by reading some of my blogs. She said we were cut from the same cloth. Her words to me were kind and lifted my spirit that day. I read her book over Labor Day weekend, which reminded me in many ways of my first book, *Reflections.* You might want to add *From Heart to Hand* to your list. I love the cover, too.

Thank you, Kristin Horvath, for interrupting my thoughts and bringing a breath of fresh air in the midst of a heavy time. She called it a "God wink." And I believe it was.

This was written and posted as a blog in September 2017.

CHAPTER 38

A Blog of Emotions

I t was a busy spring for me. After five years of working on
Mother's story, I finally had pushed it off to the publisher and
celebrated with a trip to spring training and the great Southwest.
When I returned, there was something else to focus on: my son's
June wedding. So, I enlisted the help of one of my best friends
to help me shop—dress, jewelry, and shoes for the mother of the
groom. (I hate to shop.)

Success!

Cathy and I have been friends for over three decades. You
might recall a blog I wrote three years ago when I helped her
move from Kansas City to Ketchikan, Alaska. What an adventure
we had.

Last August, I helped her move back to Kansas City. She had
mixed feelings about returning. She longed to be two places at
one time.

It was nice to have her home. We went to Royals baseball
games and visited friends, and she helped me get ready for the
big June wedding. As always, she encouraged me with my writing
and celebrated with me when I learned that, while waiting for
some final edits to be made to my soon-to-be-published book,

a short story I had submitted to a magazine four years earlier would be published.

And then the day was finally here—June 25. It was an unseasonably warm, windy day, but the wedding was beautiful. There was much to be thankful for and to celebrate.

After a joyous reception, I dropped off Cathy at her home. Before I could say the usual "Call me when you're safe inside," she adamantly asserted that she was *not* going to call me. We both laughed.

Less than twelve hours later, Cathy had departed this life without notice, without warning. Gone.

I went back and read Ecclesiastes 3 again. I had experienced verse 4 all within a twelve-hour period, *a time to weep and a time to laugh, a time to mourn and a time to dance.* I didn't have time to bask in the afterglow of the wedding.

Then, a few days later, my world of emotions seemed small in comparison to a national tragedy, injustices all around. I want to scream, can we all simply use common sense? Let truth reign! Can we pray for the wisdom of Solomon?

They say it's all part of life, and we find a way to go on. Amid tragedy for a multitude, my personal hurt is still very real, my personal joy is still very real. Individually I want to do better and be better, and collectively maybe we can make a difference in our country. At the end of the day, I think I will ask if I have loved today.

> Love is patient, love is kind. It does not envy, it does not boast, it is not proud. It does not dishonor others, it is not self-seeking, it is not easily angered, it keeps no record of wrongs. Love does not delight in evil but rejoices with the truth. It always protects, always trusts, always hopes, always perseveres.
>
> —I Corinthians 13:4-7

And so, here I am two weeks later. I miss my friend. I'm not sure the hole will ever completely close, but I did watch the mother/son dance video from the wedding and smiled. I wait to turn the pages of *Helen's Heritage* and see a version of "A House, A Home" in a national magazine—both in only a couple of weeks. And this morning, I will return to the office and hope that the office is still there. Why?

Because life, for some of us, continues on.

This was written and posted as a blog in July 2016.

CHAPTER 39

The Journey Home

It was your birthday week, and I can't believe you were not here. I remembered your birthday week last year. After living your dream of moving to Ketchikan, Alaska, and living there almost three years, you felt you needed to move back to Kansas City. I helped you drive to your new home in 2012 (what a dream trip that was), and now it was time to help bring you home. I had two connecting flights and would travel all day, but it was a spectacular, clear day in August, and I captured a beautiful snapshot of Mt. Rainier on the flight approaching Seattle.

I thought back on our trip to Seattle the year after you moved to Ketchikan. We gathered together in Seattle in 2013. We had a wonderful extended weekend visit. The three of us had been friends for about thirty-five years—Cathy, Debbie, and Debbie.

You once told me it was after that trip that you felt a little homesick. And then your health declined, so you decided to move back to Kansas City to be closer to family and doctors. But your emotions were split. You loved Ketchikan, too. You made sure that I saw the amazing beauty of Ketchikan when I arrived the second time. We awakened early the morning after I arrived to explore the landscape via a water tour, we walked a rugged beach another day, and then you drove me to breathtaking Salmon Cove, a place I long to escape to and write.

In a couple of days, it was time to begin the long journey home—two days on the ferry and then a three-day road trip traveling in the same little red car we drove on our first adventure.

We had a pleasant and uneventful drive from Washington to Kansas City—unlike the deer-hitting adventure of three years earlier. We did have one hazard on our last day on the road, but you dodged it beautifully. I'm still trying to figure out how a pig was sitting smack-dab in the middle of the interstate in South Dakota. We laughed till we cried and couldn't believe our eyes. Imagine that—a pack of deer in 2012 and a pig in 2015, both in South Dakota.

You settled into your condo in Kansas City on your birthday. It was good to have you home—spur-of-the-moment visits, Royals baseball games, shopping, and helping me prepare for the wedding the next summer.

Finally, it was the wedding day. Then the following day, you were gone. We were called to the hospital, but you really weren't there. A machine kept you breathing for another day, but you had already found peace that had eluded you much of your life.

Now, your birthday has passed again. As the weeks turn into months, I miss you more. I thought we would have more time for those Sunday afternoon visits. I went on one this past Sunday without you. I would like to hear your comments and review of *Helen's Heritage*, but your voice is absent. I still look for you on the couch when I reach the bottom of the stairs, but you are never there.

I am beginning to understand that on this side of heaven, the chair will forever be empty. So, I have this one request: "Please, save one for me there."

This was written and posted as a blog in August 2016. The summers of 2016 and 2017 were full of loss and change. The images at the end of the story are significant and inspired this blog. The one taken by someone standing a distance away wanting to capture the father/daughter dance unknowingly also captured the empty chair, insignificant to everyone but me. Why? Because it was the chair Cathy was sitting in that evening, and I remembered when she excused herself to go to the restroom. And that is one way a blog is born in my heart and head. Every "thing" is a story if we have eyes to see.

CHAPTER 40

How Many Days?

Thoughtful, considerate, devoted, caring, advisor, friend—
these are some of the words used to describe him then and
now.

A couple of months ago we gathered to celebrate our fortieth
high school class reunion. How can it be that forty years have
passed, and how can it be that someone who seemed healthy and
whole, sporting his high school football jersey only a few months
ago, has been taken from us with little warning?

He worked the land that he loved. He made room in his
barn to build our float for the parade. When chatting in a small
group that sunny afternoon, he thoughtfully asked if those of us
from out of town needed a place to spend the night. Caring and
considerate, yes, his good character shone as bright as the sun
that day. We chatted about the friendship our mothers shared.
I remembered back to our twentieth reunion. We had not had
the opportunity to speak that evening, but as I left, he caught
up with me at the door and told me how nice I looked, that the
years had been kind. It's odd, but I do remember what I wore
that evening—a pink column dress with pink pumps. My hair
still draped down the middle of my back, but I had pulled it

back in a French braid. A few streaks of gray gathered from my temples to join the back braid. We all had aged, but he took the time to greet me and say something special. I think that's why I remember.

He was not the first of our classmates to leave this life, but I think we feel this deeply because of the recent bonding at our gathering. And at this stage in life, we have come to realize those things that are most important. There is no need to try and impress each other with our wealth and knowledge. Those things are temporal. This journey on earth is for only a moment, but we want to yell, "Come back!" While death may separate us for a while, relationships are eternal.

Our days here are limited. How can we know the number?

Yesterday, I hugged my eighty-year-old mother a little tighter. I told her I loved her. I slid into the seat of my car and headed down the interstate to continue my life. Why? Because that's what we are to do, and I prayed for wisdom to understand my days (Psalm 90:12).

Life is too short to live in disharmony, bitterness, and strife. I want that out of my heart. Love and forgiveness are important every day. And I like that song … "I Hope You Dance."

Rest in peace, my classmate and friend. Until we meet again, I will remember to love and dance when I get the chance.

Lord, what are human beings that you care for them, mere mortals that you think of them? They are like a breath; their days are like a fleeting shadow.

—Psalm 144:3-4

This was written and posted as a blog in September 2014.

CHAPTER 41

Seasons Change

I t's been eleven years.

Many of our coworkers gathered in the board reception room to wish us farewell. I had been there a decade, and Vicki had spent her entire career there. It seemed surreal that we were leaving a fortune 200 company. We loved our positions, but the company was unstable, spiraling downward. We had opportunities elsewhere. Surely this would be my last career change. Deanna handed us both a box with identical gifts inside and commented, "This is a little something for you to remember it was in the fall of the year, as the leaves change, that your life changed—a new beginning."

I hadn't worn it for a few years, not since I donated the brown suede jumper. The brooch pinned perfectly on the left underneath the shoulder seam of the jumper—three leaves draped over one another: brown, gold, and autumn orange. I wondered if I could find it and then wondered if there was something in my closet I could accent with this brooch. I needed to wear this; I needed to remember. Here we go again—change, and it happens to be the same time of year another decade later.

I don't know why I get weepy this time of year, a little uneasy. I love the change of seasons, love the crisp weather and beautiful fall colors. But it seems many of life's changes have come in the fall for me. Change is an opportunity and can be exciting but also pushes me out of my comfort zone. Anxiety waits at my door. Making apple butter calms me. I don't know if it's the all-consuming attention required, manual labor process, or simply feeling the reward of completing a task the way my grandmother did. But this year is too busy for that therapy. I couldn't even find time to travel to an orchard to buy the apples. Instead I'm purging files and preparing for yet another change.

I looked through every drawer in my jewelry armoire and then finally found it in a small plastic zippered bag with a couple of other old pins. As I placed it on the left side of my sweater, I remembered what my coworker and friend said all those years ago.

I headed to the office for another day of winding down for change. On the way home, I stopped at a stoplight and wept. The words in the song struck a chord.

Seasons indeed passed for another decade—life's highs and lows, smiles and sorrows. I will remember the smiles. And as the leaves are changing again, I am confident that it will be okay.

This was written and posted as a blog in November 2013.

CHAPTER 42

Beautiful Roses

As I left work a little early the Friday before Memorial Day, I thought it odd that she waited at the parking garage entrance for a ride as opposed to driving. I waved, and she waved back. I thought—what a strong woman. She had battled a recent health issue but was almost through it and looked forward to retiring later in the summer. She did not make it into the office the following Tuesday but was at my desk first thing on Wednesday morning with her husband.

"Something is wrong with my vision, and I am unable to perform my job right now." She hoped the doctors could identify the cause soon so that she could return to work without too much time off (so typical of her, the iron woman). The month of June flew by, and we were optimistic that a specialist in St. Louis would be able to help. She had an appointment on the 8th of July. But the weekend before that, she was admitted to a local hospital with more severe symptoms. and by Tuesday, the prognosis was fatal. We visited her in the hospital and could not believe what we saw. How could this be? How could this have happened over the course of a few weeks?

She loved roses and nurtured her own beautiful ones. She frequently shared them with us at the office. When I shopped that week, the entire front of the grocery store was full of roses—all colors—as it was their annual rose sale. Thinking of her, I bought eighteen yellow-orange ones—some of her favorite—and placed them around the office. We waited for the impending sad news.

She left this life on July 27, a month short of the time she had hoped to retire. Her devoted husband of forty years, the rest of her loving family, and we (her work family) could do nothing to prevent it, although we did pray. She touched us all. I traveled to St. Louis for her memorial yesterday and was presented with a rose in her memory.

I hoped it would survive the four-hour trip home. There was a lesson to be learned from this rose. I needed to reflect more on life—hers, mine, and ours. So here I go again adding up score—Daddy got sixty-seven years, Eileen sixty-five, Bernie seventy-two, Grandpa ninety-seven, Cheryl forty-eight, young Cameron only eighteen—what I really want to say is, "Stop it!" I want everything to be fair and just. I commented to a friend, "We better hurry up and retire because we might not make it that extra year, two, or five."

I remember a mentor of mine saying many years ago that as you become older, you begin to suffer losses (speaking about death of loved ones and friends). It is the natural order of things, and we who remain must deal with it. She was the age I am now and was experiencing this difficulty. It seemed so very far in the future that *I* would have to deal with this thing called death. An even greater difficulty is dealing with untimely, premature death. But my mentor offered wise counsel that I was reminded of by my friend this week: "We must live each day the best we can in peace and love because we may not all make it to that appointed day in our understanding of retirement."

My rose made it home. I will remember Eileen and will do my best to make each day count because today could very well be *my* last. Thank you, beautiful rose lady, for gracing my life these past six years. I will never see a rose as simply a beautiful flower again. It will remind me of you and will remind me to appreciate each and every day. And, yes, I will take time to smell the roses while I can.

> Our days may come to seventy years,
> or eighty, if our strength endures;
> yet the best of them are but trouble and sorrow,
> for they quickly pass, and we fly away.

—Psalm 90:10

This was written and posted as a blog in August 2013.

CHAPTER 43

Oh Well Again

What to wear? In the scheme of things, it's an unimportant decision we face every day. It's the Christmas season, and I hadn't worn that red sweater with a tinge of sparkle yet. Good, decision was half made. Would I wear one of my black skirts or black slacks with it? No worries, I could decide that in the morning. Little did I know it would be an "Oh Well" week.

As I rifled through the hangers, trying to select the lucky black skirt, my eyes caught you—that familiar striking print, bold red roses fully bloomed with green leaves strewn amongst them on a bed of slick, black fabric. Yes, you're perfect with the sweater and for the season.

After all these years, you're still an eye-catcher as I confess your age—twenty-eight years. I purchased you within a year after the birth of my first son. A solid black sweater with a single red rose crocheted off the shoulder of the V-neck accompanied you. The scarf made from your same fabric completed the ensemble.

I wore you and wore you and wore you—year after year, baby after baby—until about ten years later when the sweater suffered a fatal hole. You survived and sought out other tops with which to partner. The elastic eventually disintegrated until it no longer gathered at the waist. No problem though, for my waist had grown, too.

O skirt of mine, who would have guessed that you would still be with me all these years later? Why, when the flouncy godet skirt left me after only two years? Why and how have you endured the stresses—the washings, the stretchings—time and time again? And yet you gradually drip dry when I wash you and wait for your next opportunity. This I do not understand and cannot comprehend. But you are still here, and so you continue with a different sweater. And others adore you. They do not know what you have endured.

At the end of the day, I received sad news. My great-niece's and nephew's mother lost her battle with cancer. She was only thirty-nine years old. My heart was sad for her and for them. I don't know about you, but in my earthly, carnal mind, I try to understand life and times, reasons and whys, even though we're not going to understand these things this side of heaven. As I've said before, I can't figure this all out. So, what do I do?

O skirt of mine—off with you! Go in the wash yet another time. Let's see if you survive as I place you on the hanger to drip dry one more time. I wished for my godet skirt. Two days later, you were still in that spot, fully dried. You survived again!

And more sad, senseless news came later that morning. All those young ones—innocent ones—are gone, executed in the comfort of their own school. They are not guilty. Why are they taken from this earth, and yet I remain?

And so, I look at you, O skirt of mine, and know that you are still here and that I will wear you once again. Why? Because there is still life in you. I will step into you yet another time. I will slide you up over my hips and gather you together with a safety pin. And no one will ever know. The sweater will cover you, and we will walk slowly at first—one foot in front of the other—one day a time.

Oh well, indeed. We don't understand why. We pause, pray, and reflect. And then, for those who remain ... life continues on.

Teach us to number our days,
that we may gain a heart of wisdom.

—Psalm 90:12

This was written and posted as a blog in December 2012. It reminds me of something from my high school literature book where you are left trying to figure out the thoughts and feelings of the author. The chapter title "Oh Well" is a term I picked up several years ago to identify an untimely, premature death, which will be explained in a future book, God willing—one of those projects still on my shelf.

CHAPTER 44

Jump for Change

COMPELLED—TIME FOR A CHANGE

Sometimes I feel compelled to do things which involve travel—like attending the wedding of a friend's daughter out of town to present her with a special gift, going to New York for a holiday concert over a weekend simply because my favorite piano player wasn't stopping in Kansas City that year, or taking a specific cruise to listen to that same piano player again, to name a few. I don't usually know exactly why, but if I am compelled, I can assure you, I will find a way to go. Other times, I simply *want* to do things, and I may feel there is a purpose—so I go with the flow and see what comes of it, even though I may lack that strong compulsion. Reflecting as time goes by, I may see the purpose—or not—and then simply am thankful for the time I had.

Recently I really *wanted* to take an extended trip to Colorado—to see parts of the state I have never seen before. I needed time away from the office, away from two jobs, and time to put life into perspective. And I was somewhat compelled to try to find Mountain Bird Ranch and pay tribute to fellow storyteller and songwriter, Dan Fogelberg. So, a couple of weeks ago, a friend indulged in my *want*, and we headed west on I-70 for a road trip.

After crossing the state line into Colorado, rather than heading toward Denver, we headed south toward Colorado Springs and arrived in time to take the last train (Cog Railway) up to Pikes Peak. I had never been there; it was majestic and amazing. I became a little dizzy once on the very top but avoided extreme nausea by taking advice to drink lots of water (think the delicious donuts that tasted like funnel cake helped, too). However, I didn't consider the long train ride down with no restrooms—perhaps I didn't need quite as much water. It was a bit of a challenge, but I survived. *Yikes!*

Day 2—headed southwest (mostly west) the next morning five hours to the Pagosa Springs area where we were guests for three days on a ranch (not Mountain Bird). I was in awe, again, with the majestic creation of God—the silence of the darkness at night, except for the sea of stars, that I forgot existed that seemed to be screaming *look at me, behold me.* And there was more—the hummingbird that stopped several times a day to draw from the flowers in the hanging basket on the cabin porch (the flowers didn't mind as they had much to offer), the San Juan Mountains that surround the ranch, and the sparkling, rushing river that runs through it. *My God does all things well.*

Treasure Falls was spectacular and made up for not finding Mountain Bird Ranch.

Day 5—headed north to Vail where we stayed another three days. There are no pictures of that drive as we took a mountain road with no guard rails and I was holding onto the door for dear life.

Yikes! But I think I would do it again. It was, to say the least, breathtaking. Vail Mountain was equally as beautiful, and, after a little afternoon nap, I woke up to a mother and baby moose right outside my window.

This was a wonderful, relaxing trip to enjoy and appreciate God's giftings to us. I am grateful for the generosity of others who

provided the lodging and gave me the opportunity to reflect on a time for change—another season of life ... as we headed home ...
... *until we meet again and are compelled to change.*

I'M JUMPING, TOO!

One of my very favorite blogs is "Today I Jumped" written by a friend. Sometimes I call her "Doc" because she listens, advises, and saves me a ton of dollars in counseling fees! She dared to do what her heart told her to do. ("Heart" is the softer version of what I really want to say: "*Gut.*") After appropriate preparation, she jumped from her day job to her own business.

Well, this week I'm jumping, too! My jump will be a little different, but, like her, my gut told me, "This isn't working." It's a funny thing, however. Even when we realize something isn't working, it takes guts to change because there is comfort in familiarity. We continue down a path because we have become comfortable in a routine. For me, that routine has been working two jobs for two and a half years. I wish I could say that I am better off than I was when I started this hectic schedule, but I can't. Things are simply status quo. So, I'm making a scary change—leaving what has become comfortable because my situation is not improving. This change requires sacrifice in hopes that something better awaits in the journey ahead. What I am gaining is time—time to write more and time to enjoy life. I will still have one corporate day job but am looking forward to my evenings and weekends.

So here we go, I am compelled, and it is time for change—come on, say it with me. Do it ... *Jump!*

I did, and the same God who created Pikes Peak will be there as my feet land on solid ground.

This was written and posted as two blogs in the summer of 2011.

PART FIVE

A Time to Work and a Time to Play

CHAPTER 45

Oh, That Sweater

O nce upon a time while raising a household of boys and baseball, football, and wrestling were the only things that seemed to matter, I had a Christmas wish—a wish for a simple, white turtleneck with a Chiefs arrowhead emblem on the collar. You see, I had this red corduroy jumper that I frequently wore to work on Fridays before a Chiefs game. I had a couple of white blouses that looked fine with it, but I really wanted that turtleneck to make it an official Chiefs outfit. It wasn't an expensive piece of clothing, but for some reason, whenever I was out shopping and would see the item for sale, the merchant never had my size. And when the stock was depleted for the year, the item was not restocked. I really felt it could be an inexpensive Christmas present for this devoted mother. So, I dropped hint after hint that all I really wanted for Christmas was a Chiefs turtleneck. I wondered if my sons ever heard me.

I kept hoping for that turtleneck through all those winning playoff seasons. Then one Christmas morning, I opened a rather large box to find a woven white varsity-type, over-sized Chiefs sweater. I knew it must have cost much more than the little turtleneck, so I expressed my gratitude to their dad and found a red skirt and a pair of stirrup pants that I could wear with it. *(Yes, I said stirrup pants, so you're probably getting the picture about how long ago this might have been.)*

I didn't want to appear ungrateful, but all I really wanted was the white turtleneck with the arrowhead on the collar. As I recall, I wore the sweater a couple of times and then was so disappointed when the Chiefs let Rich Gannon slip away to the dreaded Oakland Raiders that I announced at work I would not wear the sweater again until they acquired an adequate quarterback that could lead us to the Superbowl (which, by the way, Rich did the next season with the Raiders). So, while the Chiefs' management team *stood by their man*, I stood on my word, too. I did allow one of the guys in our office to wear the sweater for a United Way fundraiser office parade since he dressed up as the cheerleader and I dressed up as the player. It was a fun day, and Kansas City fans loved their Chiefs.

Eventually, the Chiefs acquired another quarterback, Trent Green, who led us to many victories, and I proudly wore my sweater. Since his retirement, we've been through quarterbacks, running backs, coaches, etc., and have now accepted our losing ways. Long gone are those glory days. I guess the winning years need to be passed around the various cities and teams, but I hope the winning wind blows Kansas City's way soon, or even the die-hard fans may not stick around. A joke surfaced around the various social media in Kansas City on Halloween entitled: "Worst Halloween Treat Ever" Two costumed-up kids were leaving a house after trick or treating with one looking down in his bag of goodies saying, *"Aw, man ... I got Chiefs tickets."*

I have never thought much of fair-weathered fans, but I fear I have become one. The decade-old sweater is neatly folded in my armoire, perhaps awaiting another day. I might stop and tan on my way home from work rather than rushing home to watch the Chiefs on *Monday Night Football*. The Chiefs have moved on, and so have I after all these years.

Thus, if my adult sons happen to read this, please know that a Chiefs turtleneck is no longer on my Christmas wish list.

Gourmet coffee, decadent chocolate, or a simple hug with dinner will do. My red corduroy jumper no longer hangs in my closet, so that white turtleneck simply doesn't seem to matter.

And as I say ... life continues on.

This was first written and posted as a blog in November 2012 and then reposted with a few updates in November 2018. Much can happen in six years. The sweater lives on, as do the Chiefs.

CHAPTER 46

The Way We Were

I went to my first Royals baseball game of the season last week and, oh, the memories that were stirred. I've loved the game my entire life. When I moved to the Midwest with my family from California at the age of ten, I remember being a die-hard Dodgers fan along with my dad. It took a year or two to be converted to a Cardinals fan. But then, much to the dismay of my cousin Benton, who moved the same time we did, I finally converted ... the days of Bob Gibson, Steve Carlton, Orlando Cepeda, Lou Brock, Tim McCarver, and Joe Torre. I knew the lineup, and I knew them all. One of my dreams was to someday attend a professional game. I wanted to play baseball instead of softball, but that wasn't allowed.

I settled northwest of my southern Missouri home as an adult—in Kansas City—and finally converted to a Royals fan. What a fabulous team they had in "the day" ... George Brett, Frank White, Willie Wilson, Hal McRae, Dennis Leonard, Bret Saberhagen, Paul Splittorff, Amos Otis, Dan Quisenberry, Charlie Leibrandt, John Mayberry, and Fred Patek ...to name a few (or a lot). In those days, you had to purchase tickets far in advance simply to get nosebleed seats, unless you were fortunate enough be a season-ticket holder.

Being the early days of my career, that seemed an impossible feat, but I thought, "Maybe someday when I am more established." I attended my first professional game with my dad and sister at Kauffman Stadium, then known as Royals Stadium, in my early twenties. I remember being invited by a friend a couple of times to sit with her in her mom's company's season-ticket seats—a few rows back above the third-base dugout. What a treat! I watched the kissing bandit make her way down the aisle past us and onto the field to "lay one on" George Brett one of those special Sunday afternoons (eventually that came to a halt), and I remember Mr. & Mrs. Kauffman leaning out from their suite window, waving to the crowd between innings, Mrs. K waving her white hanky slowly back and forth like the royal lady she was.

Oh, yes, the white hanky ... well, this is the way I remember the invention of the "rally rag." Perhaps someone came up with it before then, but this is my recollection of the first time in Kansas City. I was listening to the game on the radio one evening. The Royals were down a few runs late in the game. We were closing the gap, and maybe there were even two outs. I remember the announcer saying Frank White had picked up a towel in the dugout and waved it around to get everyone pumped up. Well, it worked, and it spread like wildfire. Fans and players alike started waving anything white they could find. The Royals did come back and win that game and, thus, marked the debut of the rally rag.

Yes, those were the days. It was acceptable in those days to even skip the last part of the church service on Sunday morning if you were lucky enough to have "those" seats for an afternoon game.

How fitting it was that the year my first son was born, the Royals finally won the World Series. He was four months old when I spread out a blanket on the living room floor, dressed him in his #5 "George Brett" suit, and we watched the final game. I had entered my name in the selection process that year to buy American League playoff tickets and was present at game three on a Friday night when George hit two home runs.

I tried desperately to describe those days to my sons several years later when the Royals struggled to stay out of the cellar.

The boys simply couldn't imagine. They were busy playing the game themselves—and so was I, managing two of their teams and traveling across the country with another one playing on a hotshot team. You couldn't live in our house and not play baseball. We played baseball spring, summer, and fall with a brief break in the dead of winter. We had a batting cage in the backyard and practiced in a cave in the winter. Our bags were full of bats and gloves of all colors, shapes, sizes, and impressive names—the latest and greatest. And, of course, it was acceptable to wear your baseball uniform to church if you had an early afternoon game on Sunday.

One time a co-worker told me, "I know you have great faith and God is number one in your life, but baseball is running a close second," (as he positioned his left hand about an inch under his right). Another co-worker a few years my senior, who was well past the baseball days of her sons, told me, "There is life after baseball, and it will be okay." I couldn't imagine that when I was in the midst of it all.

When I was sitting back last week, taking in the sights of the renovated Kauffman Stadium, I couldn't help but reflect on those good old baseball days. I wonder if the Kauffmans would approve of all these changes. Would they like the seats that took over part of the outfield fountains? (I think Mrs. K would be glad to see they didn't remove the fountains completely.) I think they would like that we still boast the crest—a crown scoreboard bigger and better. Those lights engulfing the circumference of the field flashing any stat or information you might want to know are quite impressive. I think they would love the natural grass infield and outfield. The blue seats are more appropriate for our team name, and I think they would be pleased to know that the original orange seats are now used at a local high school. Maybe they would have dinner from time to time in the Crown Club and maybe even take a seat in the front row behind home plate on occasion. They would likely be bombarded in the Diamond Club, so I doubt you would see them there. Would they mind that "Thank God I'm a Country Boy" was replaced with "Friends in Low Places?" (Not sure about that one.)

Being the entrepreneur that he was, Mr. K would probably understand that there is a time and season for change, and I know they would be proud to host this year's All-Star Game. I remember one of my favorite quotes from Mr. K went something like this: "If you want to become a millionaire, be a billionaire and buy the Royals." He lost money for the greater cause, the benefit of the residents of the greater Kansas City area—the continued presence of a major league baseball team. I, for one, am thankful for all of the Kauffman contributions to the Kansas City community that continue to this day and hope that the stadium will forever be called "Kauffman Stadium" because that's what it truly is.

My sons are grown now, and my life today is different—a demanding corporate career, writing, attending the ballet in the new magnificent Kauffman Center for the Performing Arts, an evening of ballroom dancing once or twice a week, an occasional dinner out with family and friends, and a concert or ballgame a few times per year. And I love that girl time with sisters and close friends.

Then I see that mother struggling to juggle everything. She loads her gang into the SUV, drops one off at a practice as she drives another to a game. If she's lucky, she might actually get to see the entire game if she can arrange a ride for the one at practice. And then she chooses her days carefully when asking to leave work early in time to see at least a few innings of her high school son's game that starts at 4:00 p.m. And hopefully she arrives in time to see the game of his life hitting a ball 400 feet against the wind to propel his team to victory or watch him strike out the side to shut the other team down (or perhaps she is lucky enough to have someone capture the moment she missed frame by frame on camera). I have empathy for her but can say without reservation: *There is life after baseball, and it will be okay!*

… love the game and life continues on …

This was written and posted as a blog in May 2012.

CHAPTER 47

The Way We Are

I remember what I wore—soft corduroy plum slacks, a multicolored sweater vest, a plum tweed with a bold royal blue wide patch of threads running through it. The silky, royal blue blouse tied it all together. My mother was happy to watch our four-month-old son while we enjoyed a rare evening out. First stop was the restaurant at the high-rise hotel across the street, great seafood that night. It was a crisp October evening, and I couldn't have been more pumped. It was exactly where I wanted to be and the only thing I wanted to do right then. I had planned for it carefully. With a little luck, my dream was unfolding. The year was 1985.

The stadium rocked every night during the regular season. It was difficult to buy tickets except for upper deck, in advance, and many games were sold out. I dreamed of someday affording season tickets, but we were starting careers and had a large mortgage. Money was allotted for our home, and that was the right thing to do. So, several times a year, I purchased upper deck tickets, and a couple of times a year I was lucky enough to use company season tickets or to be treated by a friend who had the same. I loved baseball and loved the Royals. I remember the Royals' first appearance in the World Series—1980. My boss was given a corporate suite to fill and use. I watched as my senior co-worker walked out the door early that one day. She was selected to go. She cared nothing about baseball, and I wondered if she even knew which team the Royals were playing that evening. Oh well, I watched from home and accepted that seniority and age come with privileges. After all, I was a young, confident twenty-some-thing whippersnapper and would have many more opportunities. She was sixty-something.

Five years later when the post season rolled around, I decided I would see if I could buy tickets and not depend on someone to treat me. Things were done differently in those days. I remember sending a check (or possibly money order) in the mail with a request for the American League Championship Series. You were permitted to request only one—either World Series or League Championship Series. There were no guarantees, and selection was random. Since our track record was not good to actually get to the World Series, I opted for the League Championship Series and waited. I can assure you that I crossed all the Ts and dotted all the Is. I was elated when I received an envelope in the mail with two tickets instead of a refund, upper deck down the line between first base and right field—game three—Friday, October 11, 1985. Little did I know the historic game I would be privileged to see.

I remember one of the players saying at a pep rally before the series started to never give up. "If the team loses a game or two, don't give up on us. We'll be back."

That was prophetic. The Royals dropped the first two games in Toronto but came home to a hungry hometown. And George Brett delivered the game of his life. It was a thrilling win to wit-ness. George went 4 for 4 with two home runs, and the Royals won 6-5. The "Royals" chant echoed through the spiral ramp on the way out. Everyone knew that, finally, it was our turn to win it all. And we did. I watched the remainder of the post-season games on television. We did not expect it to be the last World

Series win, and we certainly didn't expect 1985 to be our last post-season appearance for three decades.

Life goes on. I had two more sons. And, yes, they all played baseball. The focus was on their game while the Royals struggled, and struggled, and struggled. We attended a few games a year, what we could manage around their own baseball schedules, but they didn't know the excitement of those winning years. Company tickets were easier to come by.

Fast forward to September 18, 2014. I'm sitting at my computer in a virtual window waiting for my chance to buy post-season tickets. (My middle son explained how it works now.) I don't know if I will actually buy if the opportunity opens up. I know they will be expensive, and the choices limited. The telephone rings. It's my youngest son, frustrated that the site isn't working properly and wondering if I can drive out to the stadium to purchase tickets for him since he's three hours away. (I decline.) He laughs when he finds out I'm going through the same thing. "You *are* my mother." My oldest son living far away in another state is still a loyal Royal and wonders if anyone's getting tickets.

In about a half hour I learn that the youngest finally succeeded in purchasing two tickets as did the middle son, both upper deck. I hope they get to use them and get to feel the excitement that I felt twenty-nine years ago. The "Let's Go Royals" chant has meaning this year for the first time in their lifetime. It's been a fun season, and "it ain't over till it's over." (Yogi)

I haven't told them yet and they haven't asked, but Mom splurged. She has three tickets and pretty darn good seats in the lower level, just in case. After all, seniority and age come with privileges.

WINNERS

The names are Gordon, Butler, Shields, Holland, Perez, Hosmer, Aoki, Escobar, Infante, Dyson, and Duffy—to name a few. They didn't believe the bad report—that they were destined to lose.

They played like they knew they could win. Sure, there were ups and downs, but they never acted like losers.

Now for a few other present-day names: Moustakas, Davis, Herrera, Cain, Ibanez, Vargas, Duffy. And let me say, it warmed my heart to see Guthrie interpret for Ventura during an interview after a clutch win last week, teammate for teammate.

Yesterday I traveled out of town for a weekend of activities surrounding a high school reunion in southern Missouri. I really did plan to "live in the moment" and leave my phone tucked away in my purse. But a friend honed in on the game on television in Kansas City started texting me little nubs about the game, so I couldn't resist and checked scores for myself—alternating between the Royals playing the White Sox in Chicago and the Tigers playing the Twins. Holy moly, our magic number was down to one. This could be the night. After the football game, we gathered at a local classmate's house for more socializing. One television was already turned on—a Cardinals baseball game. I mentioned to the host that I was checking the score of the KC game, so he tried to find it, to no avail. Oh yeah, we *are* in Cardinals nation this far south. How could I forget?

By now, anyone and everyone knows that those boys in blue did it. We have secured, at the very least, a wild card spot. It would have been nice to see that celebration live, like George Brett. (Was he excited or what?) I watched the replays this morning.

Wild card—nope, that wasn't around in 1985. Heck, Sluggerrr wasn't even born until 1996! Wild card, division champs—it's all post season. There's a chance my sons will get to use their upper deck, game one, tickets.

This year, for the first time in many, many years there was a new song in the house. "Don't Stop Believin'" replaced "Friends in Low Places". The fans picked it. That makes me go, "hummm". The new thing I see this morning: "We're Gonna Party Like It's 1985"—I like that too.

For the first time in twenty-nine years, life for the Royals and their fans (this one included) continues on …

OCTOBER'S STILL BLUE

To the surprise of many, it's still Blue October. After we secured a post-season spot, I celebrated a "Royal" lunch with one of my sons in Cardinals nation. We wore blue proudly.

The Royals won the wild card game—and in dramatic fashion—coming from behind, stealing bases, and smashing those timely hits. The hometown crowd erupted when the game-winning hit skipped sharply past the third baseman near the line—"FAIR BALL!"

That night, life in Kansas City went up a notch. There were celebrations in living rooms (mine included), at watch parties in social establishments, and in workplaces that could not shut down. As the Royals' manager well stated, "The players didn't quit, and the fans didn't quit."

The team hit the road to play the first two games of the Division Series in California. Personally, I thought if we could win one game, it would keep us in contention. In my wildest dreams, I didn't imagine the team returning to Kansas City with a two-game lead and itching to sweep. I gathered my gear for that first home game.

My sons and I tailgated with a few friends. The parking lots were crowded, people were friendly, and we all were there to witness a common goal unfold.

It was a spectacular Sunday afternoon, a blue October sky. The aroma of every kind of barbecue item you can imagine was in the air. Hatchbacks were wide open, music strummed along, fans shared food and drink, and we watched the Chiefs on television from the tailgate next door. Time quickly passed. My son brought a broom, along with many other hungry fans.

We scattered to our seats, armed with rally rags, and allowed plenty of time to get situated for the opening ceremonial rituals associated with an important game such as this. I agree with a friend who said, "The flyovers give me chills each and every time."

The visiting Angels silenced the home crowd with a first-inning home run, but the home team Royals took control and did not relinquish the lead once attained. Again, the boys in blue would not quit. Hit after hit, play after play, they did not disappoint their fans. The visiting team went home, and the Royals and their fans "partied like it was 1985!" They (we) were division champions, and I got to witness it. "Let's Go Royals" echoed through the spiral ramp down just like in 1985. Fans hugged strangers. It was a night to remember, and it would not be the last.

As we moved to the American League Championship Series, tickets were hard to find. But my excitement did not diminish as I watched from afar—rally rag, rally beads, and hope prevailed. The first two games were in Baltimore, and I left for a sisters' weekend getaway and watch party at a nearby resort. All of us were ready to cheer on our Royals!

The truth is, we might have been a little rowdy, but we weren't alone. Strangers from two wedding parties left their groups to join us in the library bar when we were asked to leave the more formal dining room. (Hey, we tried to go there to begin with, but the doors were closed. We were simply looking for a TV and a little food. Management decided to open it.)

I love the t-shirt I wore, *Party Like It's 1985*. Why doesn't someone write the song? Why don't *I* write the song? Well, someone else did, and I couldn't have said it better.

Who would've dreamed this as the season began early last spring? We won the wild card game, swept the division series, and swept the league series—it really did happen. I don't think anyone cared that we were all sleep deprived following many extra-inning games. I watched the final game in my living room. Pinch me!

Now, we wait a little longer. I'm catching up on laundry because my closet is depleted of anything blue. World Series tickets are impossible to obtain, especially at face value. At this point, it's a rich man's game. It's not so bad. I can experience the thrill from afar. This is so good for our city, and I couldn't be prouder of our team.

I can remember 1985 as memories are made in 2014. For almost thirty years, I tried to convey the excitement, the camaraderie, the full stadium—the good old days—to my sons. Now they know; they have experienced it. It's happening in their lifetime. Boys, it really is real.

One final note, lest someone be swift to judge and think that I'm concerned and way too excited over such a temporal thing: please know that I rejoice every day that my name's written down in the Lamb's Book of Life. I am thankful for life, breath, health, and a job. I pray that the entire world can live in peace.

But for right now, please, let me enjoy this ride a little longer.

BLUESY OCTOBER

Someone asked me over the weekend if I had recovered from baseball. My answer: "I'll be okay in a couple of days." It helped to watch the "Party Like It's 1985" video a few times. That always brings a smile to my face. Our city is Royal proud as American League Champions. Now it's day seven after the disappointing loss, and since everyone else has managed to move on, including the Royals as a team, I suppose it's time for me too … after these final thoughts.

So, Blue October ended up being a little bluesy. I thought for sure we had the team of destiny, like the "Miracle on Ice" in 1980. We were headed for a fairytale ending. But at the last minute, the crown jewel slipped away. I'm not normally superstitious but started a ritual with our winning streak by rubbing Salvy's bobblehead each morning. The mornings I rubbed his head, we won. If I forgot, we didn't. This ritual was successful up until game 7. In reality, you win some and you lose some.

Also, there was the disappointment of not being able to purchase tickets at face value for the World Series. I contemplated scalper pricing—even up to two hours prior to game time for game 7. But I sensed the spirit of Dave Ramsey sitting on my right shoulder whispering, *what are you thinking? This isn't in your budget, and you can see it so much better in the comfort of your own home. Save your money for that emergency. Be practical!*

What I really wanted was to be in the middle of the excitement, like someone I met recently. By trade, he is a professional photographer whose goal is to shoot in every sports venue in the USA. But I happen to think he's a fantastic storyteller. He was at game 6 and wrote an incredible story about his adventure traveling from Pittsburgh to Kansas City. He encouraged me to go ahead and splurge on that ticket to game 7, but I couldn't pull the trigger. You might understand my bit of regret if you read some of his stories about seizing the moment. At least I have my memories of the Division Championship game.

Undoubtedly there will be a few changes when next year rolls around. All of Kansas City will hope and now anticipate another Royals run. But 2014 will be a special year to remember—what a ride! *Boys, please don't wait another thirty years because I'll be dead!*

Maybe it's time for seniority and age to invest in a reasonable portion of season tickets … hmmm … that I will ponder.

But for now, a few leaves remain on the trees. There's barely enough time to tend to those apples that have been patiently waiting. The cross-stitch project sits in a bag in the corner. It's the grateful season followed by the joyful season of giving and ringing in a new year. We will remember our loves and celebrate the resurrection with some birthdays scattered between.

I am reminded …

There is life after baseball, and it will be okay!

And until the next crack of the bat … life continues on.

This is a consolidation of three blogs written and posted in September, October, and November of 2014. We partied like it was 1985, and I blogged, and blogged, and blogged about it. I did what I was told at the writer's conference in 2010—blog about what's going on in your life. And the next year, 2015, the Royals in fact won it all again after thirty years.

CHAPTER 48

Post Time

I'LL HAVE ANOTHER

Could it be true—a Triple Crown winner this year? Will we see purple and white atop a prancing chestnut thoroughbred parading around the winner's circle? I am so excited by the possibility! Why? Well, here's my story on that.

I have always loved horses. No, I did not grow up on a horse farm, and I am not an expert on horses. But I love this animal in God's creation. My paternal grandfather raised Shetland ponies, and the highlight for me whenever we visited was to ride them. I loved the names he picked for each one. My two favorite names were Queenie (that "princess" thing, you know) and Pabst Blue Ribbon (which he shortened to Pabst). Although I forgave her, I still remember the time Candy bit my stomach simply because I stroked her back as she ate. (I probably shouldn't have done that, but like I said, I'm not a horse expert. How was I to know?) I remember that it made me sick to my stomach, but it didn't stop me from loving the ponies. Grandpa hooked up his pony team to this cute little wagon for local parades—his version of the Clydesdales marching proudly.

I rode behind my cousins on gentle-natured Rockabye Red ("Rocky"—a much larger horse) through the hills and streets of a small southern California town. My lifelong best friend, Cheryl, owned horses. She was experienced and daring. I wanted to ride at a moderate, safe pace. She enjoyed coaxing a gallop, at which time I hung onto the reins for dear life.

Although I didn't see the need to *run for the roses* personally, I sure enjoyed watching horse racing growing up—the competition and admiring each one's strength and beauty. As a teenager, I watched Secretariat win the Triple Crown, which made the country buzz. What, you say, a horse racing story? Yes! *Secretariat* is one of my favorite stories because of the story behind the story of the incredible horse. I highly recommend the movie if you want to be inspired.

A friend recently suggested that I watch *Seabiscuit*—a movie filmed in 2003. Although I know parts of the story, I have never seen the movie. When I ordered it, I was impressed with this synopsis: "True story of the undersized Depression-era racehorse whose victories lifted not only the spirits of the team behind it but also those of their nation"—my point exactly! (Here I go again talking about hope.) I believe God uses things such as this to sprinkle a little joy and hope into our society. Sometimes we simply don't give Him credit for it.

Secretariat succeeded in winning the Triple Crown after a twenty-five-year drought. Secretariat was a celebrity, and the nation was proud. Who would have thought that in the same decade we would have two more winners back-to-back in 1977 and 1978 with Seattle Slew and Affirmed? I followed the races both years. The story behind the story that amazed me in 1978 was the boy jockey, Steve Cauthen. He rode like an experienced champion in his pink jacket and secured his place in horse racing history. Having watched all of the Triple Crown races in 1977 and 1978, I thought perhaps this was the new trend. But no, others have challenged without success—a 34-year drought. It seems most writers and experts believe it takes a little luck (which I prefer to call "God favor") along with determination, talent, and training.

When I watch the replays of this year's Kentucky Derby and Preakness, it's thrilling to see I'll Have Another forge through to catch up and overtake the leader. He seems to have the will to win. So, the question might be: will he be kissed with "God favor" on Saturday? Will this be the year? I smile at my grandpa's choosing of names for his ponies, and I appreciate the creativity in selecting names for the famous racehorses. This year's hopeful winner has a fun, catchy, and perhaps prophetic name.

This week is business as usual—a job to be done, bills to pay, problems to solve (some we can, some we can't), and my copy of *Seabiscuit* arrived. So, I think I'll indulge in some couch potato time, be inspired, and re-fuel my hope tank. And on Saturday, June 9, I, for one, will watch and cheer because I think it's high time for I'll Have Another to have another so that we can all have another.

CALIFORNIA CHROME

A couple years later, I am equally excited. In fact, on May 17th when California Chrome won the Preakness, I nurtured this wild idea of a dream to go to the Belmont Stakes. Could it be done? I live in the middle of the country, and Belmont Park is in New York—outside of New York City—so, it would not be a cheap trip. But I had a little vacation money set aside and thought, "Why not explore this possibility?" I wanted to witness in person what could be a history-making event. And what another incredible story we have this year of the unexpected, but now favorite, California Chrome. What an exciting day for the owners, jockey, and trainers.

Of course, I realized several things could happen that might cause one to question doing something like this: an unfortunate injury could force Chrome to withdraw like I'll Have Another two years ago, it could rain *cats and dogs* day of the event making for a miserable outdoor mess, and Chrome could lose. So, I weighed all of that and decided that if any of those things happened, it would still be an awesome experience. Since I would be in New York, why not make it a little weekend trip to catch some sights, like the new 9/11 Memorial Museum, and listen to some good jazz/blues at BB King's, especially since I had some vacation money set aside. Could I really make this happen? It would not be my first adventure. I've done things like this before after a little nudge or two ...

Then I came across an incredible story titled "One Shot."

Well, that was the nudge I needed. So, I shifted into high gear. Airfare was high but within budget. Hotels in Manhattan were expensive, but I did find a rate I could live with if I pre-paid. I knew tickets of all price ranges were still available. It took me a few days to understand the seating, which tickets guaranteed you a seat at race time, and which ones would be first come, first serve. I finally found someone at a ticket outlet who could answer my specific questions. By this time, I was near the two-week point, and I knew that I needed to book the airfare because it would skyrocket once within that two-week time frame. Also, the agent informed me the tickets would be shipped overnight express, arriving the day before the event. I needed to know where I would stay when I purchased the tickets so they could be delivered to the hotel. Oh, and about the pricing, general admission tickets were under $40, but I would have to fight for a spot at race time or arrive very early, stake out my spot, and stay put. I wanted to walk around and experience the park and all of the excitement. I supposed I would wager a very small amount simply for the experience. Sometimes I forget why most people attend races. To me, it's about the horses.

The cheapest reserved seat was $225.

Okay. This is okay. Remember, I do have the money set aside. But for some reason, I couldn't pull the trigger, and I didn't know why. In a couple of days, I felt the crunch … airfare was breathing down my neck … but I couldn't do it. Ticket prices soared and hotel deals were gone. And then …

In a few days, I was in the middle of a crisis, and my attention was focused elsewhere. I now know that's why I didn't receive the final nudge.

Like I did in 1973, 1977, and 1978, I'll be watching from my living room—they say the best seat in the house. But I really do wish I was there. I know there will be other opportunities.

So, tune in a little early; it's a beautiful day: Gate No. 2, purple and green with a jackass on the back. *(Did I really say that?)* California Chrome! Don't miss it!

These two blogs were written and posted in June 2012 and June 2014.

CHAPTER 49

Counselor

FORTY SOMETHING

It was a bit of culture shock to leave a large corporation after a long tenure to work for a small entrepreneurial company ... a telephone list by first name ... seriously? But the company was growing, successful, and professional. And many others followed.

A few months later, the counselor came on board (she, too, came from a large corporation) and developed an in-house legal department from scratch. She treated me as her equal. She restored my faith in her profession.

We were close in age. Her only son was the age of my youngest son. We lived in the same suburban school district about a half-hour drive to the office.

We shared the same work ethic. She worked hard and long hours and was driven, and the company prospered. Camaraderie was good.

We drank coffee.

... and life continued on ...

FIFTY SOMETHING

We attended our sons' games and worked on a school fundraiser together, squeezing those things into a jam-packed work schedule. She was devoted to her family and devoted to the company.

Soon those sons were driving, then in college. They had grown from adolescents into men ... overnight ... or so it seemed.

Reflecting makes me smile: like when she drove me to work after my foot surgery for a week or two and I propped my foot on the dash, the time I dropped off breakfast burritos at her house on an early, brisk Saturday morning in January for her birthday (I rang the doorbell and left before she could get to the door), and the times she treated me to lunch. And then I laugh when I remember the times she stood her ground, professionally speaking, and others scattered ... *Women Who Mean Business* ... that award certainly fit.

When my precious friend Cheryl died, I ran to her office and cried. She was full of compassion on many occasions—through death, divorce, and disaster. I am happy to call her friend.

She gave herself completely to the challenges before her. Throughout the years, I sensed the need to thank her, although I didn't always know why. She must have had my back.

She switched from coffee to tea.

So, on this day, as life changes, I have this to say: "Counselor, let the record show, you did well, the company is well, and you will be well. Yes, all is well."

> Whatever you do, work at it with all your heart,
> as working for the Lord, not for human masters,
> since you know that you will receive
> an inheritance from the Lord as a reward.
> It is the Lord Christ you are serving.
>
> —Colossians 3:23-24

She did this.
And life continues on ....

This was written and posted as a blog in September 2013 as a business farewell to a coworker whom I much admired.

CHAPTER 50

The Dance, the Dress, the Dream

My arms were full—two sacks of groceries plus the mail. I dropped everything onto the breakfast bar. A magazine fell to the floor. I stooped to pick it up and was spellbound with the cover. It was the most beautiful gown I had ever seen—a full-length champagne satin skirt draped down from a beaded bodice overlay—pearls and sequins, white and silver. How I longed for that dress, but $300 was impossible. I tossed the catalog onto the desk when my three sons barreled in.

"What's for dinner?"

Months went by. I imagined myself in that gown. My golden hair hovered over the middle of my back. It could easily be swept up so as not to distract from the elegant gown. But where would I wear the dress? My time was soaked up on baseball fields when not at work. I didn't care about the practicality of that dress in my closet, but how could I ever come up with the money? Perhaps someday my Cinderella dream would come true—to wear this flowy gown and dance at the Harvest Ball.

Eventually, I discarded the catalog. There were baseball gloves, bats, and balls to buy. Whenever an updated catalog arrived in the mail, I peeked inside. It was listed in the special occasion section but still $300. A year went by when, to my surprise, the dress was advertised on clearance for under $100. I charged it and couldn't wait to try it on as I rushed into my bedroom and shut the door the day it arrived. It was as gorgeous on me as the model—or so I thought—until one of the boys burst through the bedroom door.

"Why are you wearing that?"

"Just trying on."

I felt silly, so I hid the dress in a remote closet in the basement. Several years passed. When I exchanged a few items in the closet to go along with the seasons, I wondered, "Should I keep this dress? Will I ever get to wear it?" The words "Do Not Remove This Tag" still hung from the inside.

A decade later—sons grew up, a divorce after thirty years—and I needed to find my way. I had to dance and enrolled in ballroom dancing classes, no longer afraid to live my dreams. Several months later, although I was still a novice, my teacher coaxed me to perform in a public routine, a waltz showcase. We rehearsed for months. A few weeks before the performance, my middle son returned home from college for the summer and was struck with cancer. I said I would withdraw from the program. But three weeks later, he had recovered from surgery with a good prognosis, and it appeared I could dance—only a few days away.

I ran to the closet, sifted through the sandwiched dresses, and found it—my perfect, sparkling dream. I took it out of the clear plastic bag, snipped off the tags, and stepped into the dress. My oldest son zipped it up, and I modeled it around the house. When I turned to head back downstairs, the sixteen-inch zipper split! I could not consider another dress. Everything was planned—the jewelry, the nails, the shoes—it had to be this gown. The performance was the next evening. Could I save my dream?

The next morning, I telephoned every tailor listed online. I found one who agreed to help if I could get the dress to her immediately, but I couldn't leave work. My baseball-mom friend Jan delivered the dress in her engine-blowing suburban, and they shared a chuckle about my obsession.

Dress in tow, I arrived at the studio early and adorned myself—the gown, rhinestone necklace, bracelets, earrings, and the glitter-filled white nails. I'm not sure which had more bling—the beaded bodice or my skin. My hair, still golden, did not have to be swept up. I learned that shorter hair helped me age with grace. I gazed in the full-length mirror and felt good. My heart pounded from anticipation and nervousness as the emcee announced my name. My teacher waited at the door; my moment was at hand. Adrenalin transformed into confidence the instant my silver shoes touched the wood floor. The skirt flowed with each rise and fall; the bodice glistened with each twirl. And I couldn't stop smiling as we waltzed without missing a beat.

At the encouragement of my friend, Cathy, this was written as an essay contest entry under the title "The Evening Gown that Changed my Life" for *ELLE* magazine the summer of 2012. This was a learning exercise to condense my story down to a maximum of 750 words. There was so much more to tell. Although it did not win the contest, I posted it as a blog with a link to the dance video under the title "The Dance, the Dress, the Dream" in June 2013. I still enjoy watching the video today and reading the comments.

CHAPTER 51

Once Upon a Time

I f you wander over to my "About" tab on my website, you will discover my "Princess" syndrome. I believe I was born with "Princess" in my spirit. As a little girl, sometimes I wondered if the stork dropped me off at the wrong house. It seemed to me I should be living in a castle and wearing beautiful, flowing gowns. (I had a vivid imagination as a child.)

My favorite fairytale was Cinderella. What a magical story it is. My favorite part, of course, is when she finally gets to go to the ball and is adorned with a beautiful gown for dancing the night away with Prince Charming. Most days, I was either pretending to be a princess or pretending to be a ballerina. Cancans with stiff tulle were popular in the early '60s. That was the closest thing I could find to a tutu in my closet. I had a few of these cancans in different colors, so I had a change of costume when my imagination would take me to an acclaimed theatre dance floor and I would be the star of the featured event (which happened to be in a back bedroom with the door shut when no one was paying attention).

You might ask: why didn't you simply take ballet lessons? Well, I was born with a few physical issues from difficulty in childbirth that required surgery as an infant and then again at the age of six. My loving mother limited my physical activities during those early years to avoid further injury. So, I would "sneak" and pretend to be a ballerina in my own world. I had a grand time pretending.

As I grew in stature, my physical limitations diminished, but the dancing-princess dream eluded me throughout my lifetime—childhood, adolescence young adulthood, and motherhood. But guess what? As I approached empty-nester hood, I finally tasted a little bit of that dream.

The year was 2008. It had been an emotional year. I was spellbound by a beautiful waltz on Jim Brickman's *Escape* CD. I listened to it repeatedly—the piano and violin combination took me to another place where I could escape. I imagined a story, even though the song was strictly instrumental.

There once was a beautiful maiden who wanted to be a princess. She enjoyed her days dancing through the garden. A young man, a prince, pursued her. At first, she was not interested until he beckoned her to dance. Reluctantly she accepted. They danced, and she fell in love. They had a glorious time together until he became disenchanted and began avoiding her. Then she pursued him, and he pushed her away. Ultimately, he walked away leaving her alone in the garden where he found her.

Well, this was only a fantasy, a self-made fairytale, minus the happily ever after—that I replayed in my head every time I listened to "Winter Waltz." I shared this story with a dance teacher who choreographed my interpretation and imagination. With his help, this princess finally had her day, center stage.

Don't give up on *your* dream. It could happen!

I once knew a girl, a princess she wanted to be,
That day finally came at about the age of fifty,
The dance was the waltz, and it is here you will see.

This was written and posted as a blog in March 2012 along with a link to the dance video.

CHAPTER 52

So, You've Always Wanted to Learn How to Play Golf ...

. . . So have I. We could capture a few hours with Mother Nature, swing our cares into the wind, and walk away with a splash of color in our cheeks.

The yearning began in high school when I heard Barry White's Love Unlimited Orchestra as the intro to live golf on television. The instrumental accompanied majestic views. Fresh air, sunshine, warm breezes, scenic views—*oh yeah*!—that must be the life. Being sequestered in an office surrounded by walls of sheetrock, fabric, and metal for days, weeks, months, and years on end fueled my desire. I dreamed that someday I would learn.

In my twenties, I watched a young Tom Watson win tournament after tournament on those luscious lawns. I wondered if he would consider a female, 5'4" caddy. But, alas, we never met. I settled for living my outdoor life vicariously via television on weekends. I followed him as he competed against Nicklaus, Player, Miller, Crenshaw, and Ballesteros and watched when the other Missouri native debuted, Payne Stewart.

JUST DRIVE THE CART AND DRINK BEER

In my thirties and forties, I never found time or justified the money for lessons, but my company sponsored an annual scramble and encouraged everyone to participate.

"I don't know how to play," was challenged with, "No pressure here ... just for fun, drive the cart, and drink beer." Problem was I didn't drink beer, and weekends were crammed full because my three sons lived, ate, and breathed baseball.

But one summer in my fifties, I discovered my life had transitioned. There were no baseball games to attend. The boys were in college with lives of their own, and I was divorced. That's when I met Tim ballroom dancing. A Google search revealed he had won a local golf tournament. I soon discovered his daughter and sister convinced him to take dance lessons because they said he lived, ate, and breathed golf.

Hmmm ... interesting.

CUTE LITTLE CARTS

When the annual scramble came around at work that summer, Tim thought it would be good for me to play. He rummaged around in the basement and hauled a pastel blue and green golf bag up the stairs. "It won't cost you anything," he reasoned. "You can use these old clubs and wear sneakers. But you need to go to the driving range, practice putting, and play at least one round before the scramble."

I survived the driving range, got over the embarrassment, and felt I was a little better at putting. At least I didn't miss the ball. When we arrived at the beginners' course, I expected to hop into one of those *cute little carts*. But instead, he pulled more equipment out of the back of his vehicle. He loaded my bright pastel bag on a cart with wheels and his dull bag on another one.

"What's that?" I wondered.

"Pushcart. You get more exercise this way."

I needed more exercise, and here was my chance to learn something I had always wanted to do in the great outdoors. *Yay!* I couldn't wait to get on the fairway with my pink balls.

My biggest fear—slow play causing others to wait—wasn't an issue. The course wasn't crowded. I surmised that had something to do with the 95-degree temperature. No one was around when I missed the ball or landed in that trap filled with sand (*thank God*).

By about the 6th hole, the mid-afternoon sun scorched through my clothes. Where were the big shade trees that lined the fairways at Augusta on television? Sweat soaked through my tank top. Tim said there was a restroom on 9—sure to be a relief in more ways than one.

The next three holes were the longest of my life. I couldn't bring myself to use the restroom when we finally arrived. A *Johnny-on-the-Spot* wasn't exactly what I had in mind. But I thought, "No big deal. We're done."

Tim, accustomed to the sweltering heat, questioned if I was up to the back nine. I assumed he could tell from my brilliant red face that I was close to death, so I joked, "Sure thing."

"Great for your first outing and walking. I thought you would be done."

I didn't have the guts to tell him I was done ... *totally done* ... and kept playing. I got through the back nine with the thought of frozen lemonade in the clubhouse. But there was no beer and no lemonade and no air-conditioned clubhouse.

Tim said the scramble would be easier because many others would be inexperienced and there would be *cute little carts*.

BEGINNER'S LUCK

We started early in the morning before the heat of the day. I found a collared shirt and impressed everyone with my clubs (though I didn't have golf shoes). I paired up with my team and confessed I had only played once. After my first two tee shots, they called me a liar as I stroked it like the best of them.

Then I missed the ball several times. They were understanding and explained that it really didn't matter—only the best shot was used. They asked me to putt first so they could read the hole better. On one of the prize holes, I launched a low line drive that ricocheted off a rock and rolled and rolled and rolled—*how 'bout that*—closest to the pin! *Yep!* I won the prize, and everyone except my team members thought I was one fantastic golfer. I gave Tim the gift certificate.

The next year, I signed up again but couldn't make time to practice. I missed the ball more than I hit it and, by the end of the day, played barefoot because I slipped in my worn-out sneakers. Staff members tallied scores in the clubhouse while we lunched, and I found out I was the hero again. You see, we took first place by only one stroke. The 16th tee was surrounded by a pond. I had my best tee shot of the day and was the only one who didn't dunk the ball. Had I not executed that shot, we would have taken a penalty shot or two, which would have knocked us out of the winner's circle. Those guys, three of the most gracious guys in the pack, thanked me all the way to the bank (gift certificates again) and never told a soul the truth—that I had no idea how to golf.

TRY, TRY AGAIN

I retired from my scramble career but played with Tim at Old Kinderhook near Lake of the Ozarks one weekend. It was another humid, mid-90-degree day by the time we arrived but didn't seem as suffocating when the breeze blew into the cart. After I missed the ball, I feared holding up the group behind us, so I skipped a few shots. By the end of the round, my saturated clothes stuck to my skin. We drove the cart up to the cozy clubhouse overlooking the beautiful course—I had envisioned all courses like this. And although I still didn't crave a beer, I slammed down two frozen daiquiris with no problem.

I played one last time in the panoramic mountains of Pagosa Springs, Colorado, but again missed many shots on the back nine and eventually simply drove the cart—but, oh, what a backdrop, another breathtaking place like the ones pictured on television. I realized then that I desperately needed help with my game. I have far too much respect for this game called golf to play this way.

TO GOLF OR NOT TO GOLF

Tim, on the other hand, rolled right along. I sipped my morning coffee on the balcony overlooking the 14th tee at Sawgrass last September while he played. Then I admired the greens, flowers, walkways, and gazebo on my way to the spa.

In April, I discovered Branson offers shows, shopping, and restaurants. As I waited for Tim to finish up at Murder Rock, I gasped when I walked out onto the veranda of the clubhouse atop the Ozark Mountains and overlooked what must be God's other country.

Today, while I inch closer to retirement, have I given up on my dream to really learn how to play golf? I don't think so. I think we become old when we stop learning. While ballroom dancing exercises my mind and body, it lacks in the vitamin D category. I still want to feel the sun, see the meadows and the mountaintops, and hear "Love's Theme" swirl in my head as the breeze blows in my face.

So, I propose we consider these things: a few lessons, good shoes, a collared shirt, and an early start with a *cute little cart* in the dog days of summer. Maybe then we can say: *Shall we golf?*

At one of my writers' group sessions, I was asked if I could pick Tim's brain for a golf story because *The Missouri Golf Post* was looking for some human-interest stories to include in their publication. I smiled and said, "Oh, I think I can fill that shoe," and wrote this in 2013. It was published with very few modifications in the September 2013 issue of *The Missouri Golf Post* as a full-page spread complete with pictures, an author bio, and links to my website and social media accounts. A friend found the magazine at his golf clubhouse, saw the article, and picked up a few copies. Many people laughed, and that brought me joy and satisfaction.

CHAPTER 53

So, You've Always Wanted to Learn How to Play Golf, Part II

It's been a few months since I chronicled my golf history—or better stated, my lifelong desire to learn how to golf. I left those of us struggling with this proposition "... a few lessons, good shoes, a collared shirt, and an early start with a cute little cart in the dog days of summer ..."

Learning to play golf is still on my bucket list and not something I simply want to try a few times. It's something I want to be able to do the rest of my life, through retirement, like my ballroom dancing. Having spent the winter cooped up in the house with my foot propped up from surgery, I've had time to reflect.

COLLARED SHIRT

Last September, I promised to play a couple of times with Tim while enjoying a late-summer vacation in Destin, Florida. The last time Tim negotiated with me to play was in 2011 while on vacation in Pagosa Springs, Colorado. It was a lovely afternoon in the mountains, little wind, low humidity, and not crowded. *Thank God.* I wondered if they would let me on the course in my capped-sleeve knit shirt with a soft stand-up collar, not really the typical collared golf shirt. And I hoped no one would be around when I teed off since I knew I would miss the ball more than I would hit it. Most of the time, it seemed we had the entire course to ourselves. At the end of the round, while Tim checked out, I snuck into the pro shop to look. I was determined not to golf again until I had the appropriate wardrobe. I found exactly what I wanted—a lightweight, moisture-absorbing, sleeveless golf shirt with a standard collar, white—and they had my size.

But whoa! $70? I don't think so! I'll pick up one on my next trip to Walmart for $20, or so I thought.

It wasn't that easy. There were no collared golf shirts at Walmart, and certainly not one like I had seen in Pagosa Springs.

A couple of months prior to our Destin trip, Tim opted to play a two-day tournament with those eastern Missouri boys on the St. Louis side, and I went along for the weekend. I relaxed with a massage on Saturday but by Sunday needed the fresh air and sunshine, so I concluded I would walk the course as he played. He encouraged me to rent a cart because of the hills, especially on the back nine. He was correct. The 8th hole was near the clubhouse and practice area. I smiled when a man who had just arrived said, "If you're walking this course, you're the best athlete out here."

I walked into the pro shop to pay for the cart and browsed around to see if they carried that special sleeveless, collared shirt. They had a similar one, but the price was about the same as the shop in Pagosa Springs. I also eyed some really cool-looking golf shoes (more like sneakers) that I considered purchasing to replace my sneakers.

Not today, Deb. We came in here to rent a cart.

I snapped out of my shopping mode and paid for the cart rental. The cart was built different than the ones I had driven in the company scrambles. I was a bit embarrassed to have to ask the young staffer how to operate the thing.

Hmmm ... how many ways can you build a golf cart?

She was kind enough to show me and assured me, "You'll be fine."

I wasn't so sure. I don't know if the cart was defective or if it was this blonde operator, but I headed down the concrete trail in my cute little cart—jerking and lunging with every press to the pedal. I caught up with the guys and in a few holes was glad I had taken Tim's advice. I had no idea you could build a golf course amidst so many hills. I even helped them (Tim and the guy he was paired with) look for a lost ball—to no avail, but I was proud of Tim for finishing in third place on an unfamiliar course. Although everyone was gracious, I really wondered if the St. Louis guys appreciated the Kansas City boy taking a qualifying spot in their tournament.

I knew a shopping trip was in order when we returned to Kansas City to be properly attired on those nice courses in Destin. I hit the gold mine on a clearance rack at Dick's the week before we were to leave on vacation. After all those years of buying cleats, gloves, and Under Armour® for my sons, I finally captured a deal for me—two collared shirts and a skort—*sweet!* I posted pictures of my bargains on Facebook and boasted about trying to golf again. Destin, here we come!

EARLY START WITH A CUTE LITTLE CART

Tim had booked us two morning tee times to get a jump on the heat, and I was excited to don my new golf wardrobe. With the exception of real golf shoes, I looked the part well and was excited to play again. I followed along beside him and acted like I knew what I was doing as we hit the practice driving area before 9:00

a.m. When we moved to the putting area, a young man joined us and said he was assigned to play with us.

What? Why would they place someone with us? We didn't ask for company. No one was paired with us the last two times I played in Pagosa Springs and at Old Kinderhook.

Tim said it was because we had an early-morning tee time instead of afternoon. The course is more crowded to beat the heat in the mornings. So, I learned I can't have it all. If I want a cute little cart with an early start, plan on having company.

We exchanged the customary handshakes and introductions, and I fessed up that I wasn't a golfer and apologized ahead of time for my inability. He was respectful, friendly, and set me at ease by saying in the sweetest Tennessee drawl, "Ma'am, I'll be chasing the ball all day, too. I'm a baseball player who had to find something else to do after graduating from high school."

Well, there's something we had in common. I had raised three baseball players, and he was the age of my middle son. I thought maybe this won't be so bad … if I could only hit the ball.

I did hit some—maybe half—picked up my ball on several fairways to keep up, and sometimes simply placed my ball near Tim's on the green to putt. All in all, it was a very nice day, and I decided I could play again with Tim and someone like that cordial young man from Tennessee. We ended our round by taking a fun selfie. We were on vacation—Tim didn't shave, and I didn't wear make-up. That was the deal.

The next day, we played on another beautiful course with scenic views of the Gulf of Mexico. But my comfort level quickly diminished. I saw a couple a generation older putting on the practice hole and knew that we would be paired with them. At first, I wasn't terribly concerned since the prior day had gone so well, but I soon learned that this husband and wife team from Vail, Colorado, were seasoned golfers. I was humiliated with missing the ball which started soon after the first tee. Tim said I was nervous because they were skilled players. I only know I was uncomfortable most of the day, and if that wasn't enough, I encountered a snake in the long grass off one of the fairways looking for my wandering ball. *Yikes!* I wanted to walk back to the parking lot but knew that probably wasn't proper golf etiquette.

As I struggled, I watched that tiny lady hit ball after ball off her tees. She never missed. I wondered if that was because of the huge driver she sported. That's got to be it! I need a *big* driver like hers to solve my problem.

I thought the day would never end. We shook hands after the 18th hole. They both complimented Tim on his game, and she encouraged me in the kindest voice, "Dear, you simply need a few lessons."

To say the least, I wanted to kiss the beach once I stuck my toes in the sand when we arrived after golf. The saltwater soothed my aching feet, and the waves were music to my ears—much more relaxing than the greens that day. I vowed to never play golf again without fixing my game.

WHERE DO I GO FROM HERE?

While cooped and propped this winter from foot surgery, Tim and I strategized on what I needed. We agreed lessons were a must, and real golf shoes should be considered. I suggested that maybe I needed new clubs—or at least a bigger driver. I am grateful for the old clubs he found for me to use as I try desperately to learn this game of golf. Maybe it isn't a good idea to buy new clubs yet, but at least I need a bigger driver, one like the Colorado lady owned. He got a strange look on his face when I brought up that, and I *knew* there was a bigger driver in the basement.

Are you kidding me?

I put him on the spot. "You withheld the *big* driver?"

Tim explained that, in his opinion, the big driver is harder to hit. Of course, my theory was, and is, that the bigger the head, the more surface for contact. I learned from other experienced golfers that they shared Tim's opinion.

So, no, I haven't given up on my dream to really learn how to play golf. I've got my collared shirts, understand that I will have company with an early tee time and a cute little cart, and have new sneakers. Golf shoes and possibly new clubs will come later. So, stay tuned—as I headed out the door for my first lesson this week, Tim placed that *big* driver in my bag. Oh yeah, I can hear that sweet ping now!

I promised to write a follow-up story to my golf adventures for *The Missouri Golf Post.* Ten months after the first story was published, I found time to devote to Part II. It was featured in the July 2014 issue once again in a full-page spread with pictures and full-author credit. Having these two stories published in a widespread magazine to golf courses and their subscribers made me realize that there was an audience and a place for my down-home writing.

CHAPTER 54

Blue, Bosses, Beginnings

BLUE

As I stretched the seat belt across my blue floral-printed dress to begin the forty-minute commute to work, my mind wandered back fifteen years ago to when the dress was new. I thought it was a perfect summer work dress. I dry cleaned the dress for years until last year when I chanced machine washing it in cold water. Considering the age of the dress, it didn't seem practical to continue with the dry-cleaning expense. It survived and so did I. My life was, oh, so different in the early days of this dress.

BERNIE

To say the least, I was a bit intimidated at our first meeting. There sat one of the most respected men in the corporation, a thirty-year veteran, member of senior management, PhD in Economics, and a heart transplant survivor. He was mature, distinguished, and had grandchildren the age of my children. We worked alongside each other for the last six years of our career at this Fortune 200 company—the liaisons of a twenty-two-member board. I was there to assist him. I have many fond memories. I never heard him raise his voice. He eventually agreed that there was no need to keep a manual calendar when the electronic version was introduced. We documented the history of our outstanding farmer-owned coop, we managed the governance process, and I loved my work. He had a very controlled sense of humor. It was his idea to participate in a fundraising float parade. (All of us ended up enjoying it, although we felt we were too busy for this.)

Unfortunately, a few years later, we also witnessed the downfall of the organization. As he made plans to retire, I sought out another company. He spoke words of encouragement to me … "A new beginning, a fresh start." And, so, it came to pass.

BROOKS

I didn't know if I could work alongside him the way I had Bernie. He was so much younger—ten years my junior. After all, I was accustomed to mature bosses, professionals. And I was accustomed to large corporations. But, nonetheless, there I was beginning again. And I learned from this younger one. Soon I learned he, too, was mature, professional, and didn't require accolades of glory to perform, much like Bernie. I watched him build a company alongside the founder. I witnessed him make mature decisions and manage people fairly. He was respectful to everyone but made tough decisions when necessary. We shared a love of baseball. On stressful days, he might pick up one of the bats leaning against his office wall and swing it around. On good days, he whistled. I worked alongside him and the founder for a decade and watched as they positioned the company for a grand merger. And I watched them step down for the new leadership and a new beginning.

BEGINNINGS

This past week, as I wore my blue dress, these two beginnings came full circle at the same time. I heard that, after twenty-two years with his new heart, Bernie transitioned to his eternal home—what an amazing gift to have that many years following his transplant and to enjoy a decade of retirement. Then Brooks stopped by the office to pick up a few last things. As he swung those bats on his shoulder, flipped the light switch, and headed down the hall whistling, I was left reflecting. I was reminded of the last *Mary Tyler Moore* episode when she peeked back into the studio one last time and turned off the lights. And, so, I remembered the two "B" bosses, the blue dress, and beginnings.

And for most of us, life continues on …

This was written and posted as a blog in July 2013. One of the blog comments made me laugh. "Since [everyone] has moved on, is it time to retire the dress?" So, I did—bought a new blue dress, sent the old one to charity, and moved on to a different job.

CHAPTER 55

Vacation Diary

A friend invited me to escape the cold winter and visit her in sunny southwest Florida for my birthday. I found reasonable airfare, planned out the days, and booked it. Then I decided it would be nice to visit my son on the way down, so I added a few flights and days to the front end of the trip.

I left early on a Saturday morning, checked two bags and carried on two, changed planes in Nashville, and arrived in Pensacola without a hitch or a glitch. (Well, I did need a little help lifting and squishing my full-size carryon into the overhead bin.) I hadn't traveled by air in over a year, so it was a nice jetsetter feeling again.

My son greeted me at the bottom of the escalator with a bear hug while his girlfriend waited in the car—first time meeting her. After another warm hug, they loaded the bags into the trunk—all four. What a beautiful arrival day—the clear, crisp air and sparkling sun created a to-die-for lunch on the deck of a beachfront restaurant.

The next morning, we loaded up the car with twin three-year-old boys they were babysitting and headed out for a twenty-minute drive to church. I looked forward to attending with them, but sometimes our best-made plans simply don't work out. As he unbuckled the twins out of their car seats, I opened the trunk to gather items. To my surprise the trunk door came crashing down on my head. The blow stunned me for a second—the shock that something had hit my head really hard. Surprisingly, I didn't feel pain but, in a few seconds, found myself grabbing for tissues in my purse to stop the flood of blood streaming down my face and onto my green satin blouse. By the time my son returned to the car after depositing the twins safely in their classroom, my hair had turned strawberry blonde. He handed me paper towels and a bottle of disinfectant from a first aid kit and escorted me to the restroom to cleanup.

The service was almost over by the time the bleeding had halted and I had rinsed the blood from my hair and clothes. So, I joined my son in the lobby coffee bar where he was waiting for me. Worried, he kept asking if I was dizzy or seeing double. I was fine. Having raised three boys, I was all too familiar with the amount of bleeding that a head gash can produce. But I never expected it to be *my* head! (You might have thought this portion of the diary would have been about one of the three-year-old lads, not a fifty-something lady.)

The next three days were as pleasant as I could have imagined. We enjoyed simple things—a few meals together, watched *Frozen*, and stocked up at Walmart. I am so glad we took some time late one afternoon to visit the National Naval Aviation Museum.

I loved seeing slices of history in more ways than one.

We crossed the street to view the Pensacola Lighthouse, and paused as "Taps" played at dusk (brought back memories from a few decades ago).

Like the day I arrived, the sun glistened in the sky the afternoon that I left. Indeed, such a pleasant visit it was, but it was time to leave.

Five hours later, my friend met me at the airport and had a snack waiting when I arrived and settled into my special room. Although others may visit it from time to time, I feel very much at home when I am there and settled in like a returning college student, "my room."

The thing I enjoy the most when I visit is simple relaxation. There's no rush to be anywhere at any specific time. We eat when we want, get dressed when we want, and go out when we want—or not. I love it!

The sun greeted me on my birthday morn. And I kissed it goodbye when we left for dinner. We celebrated my birthday like royalty, in princess style.

The next couple of days, we shopped a little, enjoyed lunch on the veranda, and watched the sun dance on the water one last time.

We watched the Super Bowl and *Maleficent* at the same time (minimal dozing for me while multitasking) and one last sunset.

The next morning, as we waited to board our flight home, we overlooked the tarmac and saw security vehicles and personnel scurrying around. Passengers chattered about who the VIP might be. We were on a flight to Kansas City with a stopover in Washington DC. I recognized third in line to the throne on the front row when I boarded.

I don't believe there was an empty seat on the flight. As we began the descent into DCA, the plane rocked from wing to wing. I looked around to see if anyone else appeared worried, especially when the ground seemed close enough to jump to. I glanced over to blue eyes on my left and then to brown eyes on my right. Both were filled with concern. I wondered which wing was going to hit the ground first. I realized many others wondered the same thing when all wheels finally gripped the runway and the entire cabin erupted with applause. I later learned there was a severe wind advisory in Washington that day.

It was smooth sailing on the next leg to Kansas City. I thanked my friend for the ride home and a wonderful birthday, again.

This may not have been the adventure of a couple years ago driving to Alaska. It was an adventure of another kind. Each morning when I brush my hair to the side to cover the scar, I will remember the special time with my son, his girlfriend, and a dear friend. I wrote another chapter in my book of life. This was one of those times I had a choice and chose to dance.

And life continues on …

This was written and posted as a blog in February 2015.

CHAPTER 56

Dream It!

At one point in my life, there was nothing I wanted more than to figure skate Olympic style. Problem was, I didn't start training until I was twenty-three—a tad bit late. So, as I sit here this morning enjoying one of my favorite things these days (sipping coffee in bed) and waiting to watch a few hours of Olympic ice dancing, I remember.

A ballerina—that was my first artistic dream. I wanted a beautiful tutu, and I wanted to be the featured dancer. I think I was about four years old. I pretended in secret because of physical limitations due to a couple of surgeries. I wasn't supposed to "strain" myself in the abdomen and groin area. So, I hid from Mama and pretended and practiced on my own without formal dance lessons. I had three crisp cancans (white, yellow, and blue) that I wore with my Sunday dresses. These became my tutus. I changed my wardrobe when I changed the old 78 records on that old player. I didn't understand what "first position" was, but that didn't stop me from dancing. I dreamed it, and I danced what I felt from the music.

Did I become a famous ballerina and that star? Obviously not. But I did the little I could at the time. And life changed and evolved, as did I. Life happens as we make choices and decisions. But my love for dance, elegance, and choreography always remained.

Ice skating fascinated me as well, but there was never an ice-skating rink in the towns in which I lived. I watched Peggy Fleming, then Dorothy Hamill, and dreamed of flowing elegantly and being a ballerina on the ice. Instead, my sister taught me to twirl a baton when I was fourteen. I perfected that well enough to make the team and enjoyed the formations and choreographed routines.

And life continued on. I did a stint in the military, then focused on continuing my education and a corporate career. I squeezed in a few ballet lessons (Mama wasn't around to watch or worry), then settled in Kansas City when I was twenty-three years old.

There was an ice-skating rink—a few of them, actually. So, I signed up for adult group lessons. If I could simply learn to skate backwards ... that would be awesome. There were a few basics to learn first—like how to stop and start and how to trust the blades to hold you, the inside edge and the outside edge, balance, bending the knees, and then finally the basic 3 turn. After a few weeks, skating backwards was on the schedule. I couldn't wait. The instructor worked with each of us individually after some initial instruction and demonstration. Nothing she showed me worked. "Bend your knees, lean on the edge. Try to cross your left foot over the right as you lean."

It was hopeless. I was not going to get this. The thing I longed to learn above all else would not come easily, maybe not at all. My body didn't cooperate and neither did my brain. I stayed late during the open skate session and practiced on my own for a couple of hours to no avail. I simply couldn't get it and left my weekly Monday evening lesson disappointed. I went about my normal work week and thought that I would not sign up for the next set of lessons since I couldn't seem to get past this hurdle of skating backwards. And then, that Thursday night/early Friday morning, I awakened from a dream.

I dreamed I was skating on a highway. I was on an exit ramp that wrapped around in a complete circle. I completed a 3 turn to switch directions from forward to backward. I maintained my balance on the turn and, since the ramp was spiraling down, crossed my left foot over my right, bent my knees, leaned in deep on the outside edge of my right foot, crossed the left foot over the right, and kept going and going and going!

But it was simply a dream. My eyes opened and I was fully awake instantly. Yes, it was a dream, but it wasn't simply a dream. I felt it. I had figured it out, and I knew it. Out loud I announced, "I can do it, I can do it!" I couldn't wait to get to work and tell someone. Others didn't seem to share my excitement. But I knew I could do it. The following Monday, I sat down on the bench outside of the rink and laced my skates. I was early and excited. My instructor arrived as I tied up my last lace, and I bubbled over that I could do it. She questioned, "Skate backwards? Did you practice?"

"No. I dreamed it!"

I don't think she believed me, but I didn't hang around to explain further. I stepped out on the ice and showed her. Same as in my dream, I did an outside 3 turn and kept skating backward. And then I discovered the most amazing thing. I could skate much more powerfully backward than forward. I didn't want to stop for the lesson. I didn't sign up for additional group lessons but instead signed up for private instruction with a coach, made a skating skirt, and purchased a pair of very good customized boots (skates). I learned a great deal over the next couple of years—dance steps, spirals, spread eagles, layback Ina Bauer, a few jumps, and a few spins. I had tremendous stretch and flexibility but poor spinning technique. I knew I couldn't really compete, but it was fun to learn and dance on the ice.

I cried when Tai Babilonia and Randy Gardner had to withdraw from the 1980 Winter Olympics seconds before their performance.

And then life continued on … babies to have, sons to raise, ballgames to attend.

I remembered my dream and stepped onto the ice again twenty-five years later. At some point over the years, my customized skates were sold in a garage sale. I rented a pair and was surprised at how weak my legs were. I could barely complete a 3 turn. I stayed an hour but left when a hockey team showed up to practice. What was I thinking? I'm fifty something!

Dancing, dreaming, skating—these days I have a small wardrobe of dresses (not tutus) and shoes (not skates). I dance on a wooden floor instead of an ice rink. I dance for enjoyment and exercise. I don't compete. I listen to the music, and sometimes I fall asleep meditating on a new waltz pattern. And I know it's true: if I can dream it, I can do it.

And I cried when Meryl Davis and Charlie White won the first Olympic gold medal in ice dancing for the USA. It was beautiful.

This was written and posted as a blog in February 2014. Indeed, I am a dreamer. I dreamed I could ice skate backwards, and I did. And I dreamed I could write a book, and I did!

CHAPTER 57

A Night Out

I am a lover of music. If you follow my writing, you've probably figured out that music inspires me. However, when I try to make my own music, the result is never what I plan. I have to rely on the gifts and talents of others to fulfill this need. So, when my favorite performers visit my city, I indulge in the opportunity to see these talented musicians. Since I don't miss these opportunities, my sisters tease me ... *groupie*. Of course, I refuse to wear that label. I am *not* a *groupie*. But here's my latest little story of simply a night out ... with Kenny G.

Last August, I received a flyer from the local symphony for the upcoming pop series season. One of my favorites headlined the brochure—back in town to perform with the symphony in January, my birthday month. No more shopping required! We went online to purchase tickets (remember last August)—not soon enough for the best seats, however, for either of the two scheduled performances. We had to settle for choral loft, which is behind the stage (musicians' backs to us). The only other choice was the very top, upper grand tier, on the sides. Having been to Helzberg Hall several times, I knew there isn't a bad seat in the house but was a bit bummed that we were six months away and had to "settle" for these. I had hoped for the orchestra or parterre section. I printed off the tickets and tucked them away in a file awaiting my birthday month.

A few months later, I also scheduled a foot surgery for the first of December and really hoped I would still be able to attend the concert on January 17. I had ditched the crutches the day before the concert and felt I could leave the foot down long enough for the performance and wear my walking boot. But I did think it would be a good idea to valet park. So, I went online to buy the valet parking ticket and noticed an additional performance had been added. Seriously? I couldn't believe it. I could probably get better seats for the added performance on Sunday, but we already had Friday evening planned. I thought, "Oh well, not worth the trouble. We'll go as planned."

We arrived early, and I had a plan to buy Kenny's latest CD, wait in line to have it autographed, and to be included in the drawing for the saxophone giveaway. (He gives away one at all of his concerts.) I walked through the front doors of the magnificent Kauffman Center for the Performing Arts as the ushers were being released to man their posts and immediately saw an old friend, a retired schoolteacher who now works this seasonal, part-time job. We chatted for a moment, catching up, and she asked jokingly if I was one of those crazy fans they had been warned about who might storm the stage. A *groupie*? Not me! We laughed, and I assured her I would only take my chances at winning the saxophone in the drawing.

I was the first one to buy a CD and the first to wait in line for his autograph. I waited patiently. He arrived at the table about forty-five minutes before curtain time and autographed the CD. I said, "Thanks for coming back to Kansas City, Kenny." He smiled and said, "Sure thing." Without further ado, I yielded my space to the next person (no *groupie* here).

My foot was tiring, and the boot was a bit heavy, so I asked to squeeze in on a bench in the foyer by the southern glass wall of the modern architecture. We sipped coffee. I decided to "check-in" on Facebook and was in the middle of the post when, to my surprise, there he was about four feet from me! He had picked up the saxophone from the display table and brought it over to the light. I shifted gears quickly to snap a picture. But silly me somehow clicked away from the page before posting and lost the close-up picture. Not to be completely discouraged, I walked over to the table where he had returned and had to "settle" for a back shot.

It was time to find our seats in the loft. We took the elevator to the next floor up, and I had to negotiate a few steps down to the first row of the loft. I found our seats a few spaces in, right center. Instead of individual seats, it was a curved bench seat with a back and completely cushioned—very comfortable. And I was surprised with the tremendous view. Had I been a "real" groupie with two good feet, I surmised I could jump down right on the stage with them—all of them—Kenny, his band, and the symphony musicians. Instead, I settled into my assigned spot and observed the sheet music in the percussion section: "My Heart Will Go On." I removed the heavy boot and leaned it against the railing wall in front of me as the musicians filed into their seats. And not being a rookie or a groupie, I didn't need to see the difference in wardrobe to recognize his four band members over the symphony musicians, although that was an appropriate distinction and quite striking. (The band members were the men in black and the symphony musicians were in white.)

Maestro entered the stage floor with a warm applause, and then, from behind me, I heard the familiar sound of a horn, the soprano sax I have come to love. The vessel for this wonderful sound walked down the same steps I had taken a few minutes earlier and came to rest on—you guessed it—the front row of the choral loft! Of course, being rooted in legalism, I wasn't about to snap a picture during the performance. That is prohibited. But I certainly did enjoy all of the moments—yes, the entire song. When the song was over, Kenny traveled the entire length of the front row choral seats all the way to the other end. Oh, my goodness, he was headed straight for me, and my boot was in the way! If he (all 135 pounds) tripped over it, I could reach down and pull his ringlets. But then my sisters would be correct—I really would be a *groupie*. So, what did I do? I cleared the way; grabbed my hefty boot, purse, and scarf; and protected my bum foot as he barreled in front of me "slapping high fives" with everyone along the way. (What a moment!) We smiled as he headed down to the stage, and the evening passed all too quickly. I thoroughly enjoyed my early birthday present. Unfortunately, he did not draw my ticket out of the fishbowl. I was not the lucky one to whom he serenaded and handed over the saxophone.

My usher friend found me again as I waited for the valet to bring around our vehicle. She noticed where we sat, that we witnessed so close the impressive entrance, and wished I had won the sax. Yes, it would have been nice. But I enjoyed every note of every song and think I understand why the musicians led the way into battle in the Old Testament stories, why Gabriel will blow his horn on that all-important day, and why there is singing in heaven. And I am grateful that we have all of these things—gifted people and music—to enjoy a little bit of heaven on earth on simply a night out.

This was written and posted as a blog in January 2014.

CHAPTER 58

Earthly Treasures

Last week, I took a little birthday vacation and visited a friend in sunny Florida for a few days. We've been friends for over thirty years. She befriended me my first day on a new job with a new company when I was only twenty-three years old. We had much in common—married, no children, about the same age, and we both liked to sew. She taught me to cross stitch—a pastime that became therapy for years to come. We had children over the same time period while still working together about six years later. As life changed for us, there were periods of time where we didn't see each other frequently, but we never completely lost touch. She is one of my treasures—a lifelong friend.

She really made my week special. It was my birthday each and every night. We had a fun time along with quiet time, enjoyed sharing and reminiscing, and discovered we are still learning from each other. She set up a game for us to play together and pointed out a few more features on my iPhone. I taught her two line dances in her living room. She introduced me to a couple of her other friends, who greeted me warmly and joined us for dinner. We shared a common thread—her friendship.

One day was spent on the beach. I combed the beach, picking up seashells—something I hadn't done in years. I felt like I was on a treasure hunt as I searched for different colors and shapes. Some shells were large with distinctive colors and markings—some obviously had weathered many storms. Other smaller ones were perfect and worth keeping for their beauty. When I returned home, I took great care in cleaning my shells—soaking, drying, and finally rubbing each one with oil.

I couldn't help but correlate these shells I collected to my earthly treasures—family and friends. They, too, are a varied collection—large and small, some colorful, some plain, some smooth, some rough—but they all complement my life. I must remember to nurture these treasures that are still a part of my life and will honor the treasures who have passed on or who graced my path for only a brief moment in time but left a mark, an impression, an influence—the large and the small.

My book, *Reflections*, is a celebration of some of my treasures—relationships with friends and family. I suspect I will write a sequel or two, as I barely scratched the surface when I think about all of my treasures, including my friend of thirty years and the two I met on this trip. I never know when another treasure is going to debut in my life.

My vacation was far too short. The return flight home was packed to capacity. A lady boarding at the end sat down next to me. One might have been annoyed, calling her a chatterbox, but there was something about her that struck a chord in my spirit. She was continuing on to Las Vegas for a week with family and friends—her treasures. As I prepared to deboard that afternoon, I handed her a copy of *Reflections*. I do not know why she happened to sit next to me that day, and I do not know why I gave her a copy of my book. But somewhere in my jar of treasures, I believe she is represented.

When I look at my treasure from my day on the beach, I will remember my earthly treasures who are also my eternal treasures. I am, indeed, blessed beyond measure. Have you considered your treasures lately?

But store up for yourselves treasures in heaven,
where moths and vermin do not destroy,
and where thieves do not break in and steal.
For where your treasure is,
there your heart will be also.

—Matthew 6:20-21

This was written and posted as a blog in February 2012.

CHAPTER 59

Just Breathe

*Va-ca-tion ~ noun ~ "A period of suspension of work, study,
or other activity, usually used for rest, recreation, or travel ... "*

Sometimes I have to remind myself what vacation is all about.
It's not simply a day or two off to run errands or to take care
of personal business, although that's what much of mine is used
for. Recently, I knew that I needed a real vacation described in
the definition above, and one or two days were not going to
accomplish what I needed—a true break in order to re-group
and re-focus.

Between my corporate position and some personal issues, I
was totally drained. I had reached a point where the simplest of
tasks was a chore. I didn't feel like I was good for anything or
anyone. One night, I felt like a massive weight was bearing down
on my chest and there was no way out. I was so overwhelmed
that I sent an old friend a message and asked her to pray for me.
I didn't offer details about my situation, but she said she would
pray. When I finally fell asleep, I dreamed I was suffocating. In
the dream, she was next to me and said, "Deb, just breathe, just
breathe." That's all she said.

I woke up and realized I was holding my breath and was relieved that I really could breathe. The horrible feeling of not being able to breathe kept me awake the remainder of the night. Later that day, I read a blog where someone described a completely different situation and paused to simply say, "Take a breath." Wow—did that speak to me or what?

For the first time that I can ever remember, I scheduled two full weeks of vacation at one time. The first week was spent out of town, a typical traveling vacation—nice accommodations, the beach, the pool, completely away, and total relaxation with no schedule. I was blessed to be able to do this on a shoestring budget. The second week was a staycation—nothing exciting, but I did accomplish a few personal things, had more writing time, and took one brief day trip with my friend Cathy. I am so glad that I took that little afternoon trip with her to a small rural town. We had lunch at a cozy diner that served homemade pie. Yum! (I took time to *smell the roses*.)

The important thing is that I recognized my need. I needed the break to reset myself—a reboot, if you will. I learned that when I'm on vacation, I not only *smell the roses,* I see others and their needs. I see the person next to me stressed the way I was. I see the person struggling with a physical disability. I see the carefree spirit of a child.

One day, I watched God's wondrous creation—the ocean, the waves, the washing of the sand forward and the return. I watched a child build a sandcastle, and I watched older children battle the waves with their boogie boards. After watching for a while, I joined in with them playing in the waves. And you know what? We saw dolphins a few feet away.

No driving, no make-up, no e-mail, no schedule, no stress equals a better me!

My vacation has come to an end, but I am refreshed to go back into my world and deal with my situations and the people there. Hopefully they, in turn, can tolerate me. I think I took my vacation for me and for them.

I am not ashamed that I took time to ... just breathe.

This was written and posted as a blog in September 2012.

CHAPTER 60

Days of Labor

*How did I go from being the youngest girl
in the office to the oldest—overnight?*

In 1979, in my early twenties, I moved to the big city and launched into corporate America. I had worked since I was twelve when I started babysitting, washed dishes in a bowling alley restaurant, and then worked in a chain department store all through high school. I then had a military tenure and furthered my education, but this was now the *real deal* in the *big town*. The Royals were hot and so was I. I was confident in my abilities but not aggressive or overbearing, and certainly I avoided conflict. Above all else, I wanted to be cooperative and easy to work with. I wanted to please everyone and hear those words, "Well done!"

After a brief orientation in the HR Department on my first day, the recruiter escorted me to the fifth floor and down the Treasury Department hall to the Tax Division's office on the left side of the corridor. It was a small seven-member division, a small office with its own system/rules within a large company. There was one other lady, much older and nearing retirement, in the group, who was to be my trainer and mentor.

The first thing I noticed on my desk was a large, green glass dish with four grooves for cigarettes—an ashtray that I suggested could be removed. But I wasn't special. There was an ashtray on everyone's desk, and I soon learned that I was the only nonsmoker in the group. Marie said that, although I didn't smoke, the ashtray was needed for others as they interacted with me. Boy, did I find this to be true as the ashes grew at the end of her cigarette and eventually fell like a slinky toppling end-over-end onto my desktop. No worries, however, she quickly blew them away into the open air, and they scattered onto the floor.

Marie wanted to mold me. She wanted me to dress like her, work like her, eat with her, act like her. But I certainly had no intention of becoming like her. Although professional and well dressed, for goodness sake, she couldn't even apply her make-up properly. Underneath her large-framed glasses, I saw eyeliner smudged and dots of mascara speckled beneath her lower lashes on many days. Her hairdresser teased up her thin, fine hair colored the perfect shade of red to where you could see straight through it. Not to mention that I would never ever force my way of doing things on someone else. No, I would never become Marie. After a couple of years, I moved on to another position in the company—a very good place to be, good for my career, and out of the reach of bossy Marie. Over the next few years, I saw her in the hallways, on the elevator, and in the cafeteria. I was respectful and gave her a retirement gift on her last day. I could not hold a grudge and always wished her well, but I would *never* be like her. I never regretted my decision to move on. I had the world at my fingertips, or so I thought.

After a decade with that fabulous company, they announced plans to consolidate offices in another city. It was a sad time for the employees and the city to lose such a good company. I elected not to relocate. Instead, I embarked on those childbearing years of bottles, diapers, Disney movies, and minivans.

It was scary re-entering the workforce in my mid-thirties. I did not want to, but we needed additional income for our family of five. During the days of my job search after I had the boys tucked in bed, I stepped into the shower and let the water wash down over my head along with the tears—the fear of my life changing overwhelmed me. Furthermore, so much had changed in the workforce (a computer on every desk), and I was comfortable with my place as a mom. I thanked God for that time at home with my sons as the tears washed down the drain. I mustered up the courage, sharpened my skills, and felt fortunate that someone took a chance on me after being a stay-at-home mom for five years. It didn't take long to get back into the swing of things, and I moved on up in that corporation for yet another decade … until the company spiraled into bankruptcy.

Change? Not again! At least this time I still had skills, I had built on my experience, and the boys were older. They were busy with school and sports. I'm not sure they cared if I was home or not. I thought maybe someone would still hire an old lady in her forties.

Well, someone did. I had never worked for a start-up, entrepreneurial company. My two previous employers were established, large corporations when I started. This was something new and different. I was shocked to see the phone list—a modest two-page listing by first name. But I endured that worthless feeling the first six months and settled into my third corporate career in as many decades. I felt like I helped build the company. I watched the company go public in three different entities, watched it expand and make a ton of money while winning many awards in the city and industry. I ran the office, oversaw several building projects as we expanded, and hired a full administrative staff. My plate was overfull.

No longer the youngest one in the office, I wanted things done my way for good reason. Having had to operate with limited staffing, I could not afford many hiccups—had no time for that. I knew what worked, and I knew what didn't. I still wore and liked pantyhose with my business suits, although I did wonder if some of the girls thought it was a bit frumpy. I hoped most of them liked me and respected me even though I wanted things done a certain way. By this time, my nearsightedness had turned into farsightedness. I didn't want to admit that I needed bifocals, but I did. (Thank God for blended lenses.) I resorted to a 5x makeup mirror to apply my eyeliner to those lids that were folding down closer to my eyes. I cut my long locks to give myself a free facelift; I used various products to give my fine, short strands some texture to raise up off my scalp and hoped the scalp wasn't visible. One morning after much work on that short stuff, I reached for the hairspray to hold it all in place and, after spraying generously, realized I had the styling mousse instead. Oh, my goodness!

Then reality kicked in. The thing I feared the most had come upon me. I had turned into Marie!

In my mid-fifties, I learned what entrepreneurs do—they build businesses, and they sell them. The company I watched grow and helped build merged with another. And after yet another decade with another company, another change was about to take place. But this time it was different. I felt what many do as they approach the twilight of their career. I was a bit tired. I didn't want to be grouchy and wondered exactly how many years I had left. I watched a coworker at sixty-four, desperately trying to make it to sixty-five in order to retire, succumb to the strangest thing to attack a body I had ever heard of. She didn't make it. I thought of my dad, who died when he was only sixty-seven. I wanted time to write more, to bring those other book projects in my head from a dream or an idea into reality. I didn't want to crack the whip any longer and climb the ladder, but I wasn't yet sixty. How can this be? It's too much and yet not enough.

So it was and so it is. Finally, after thirty years, the Royals were hot again, but what about me? I moved to one last position with the founder of the entrepreneurial company and realize that many covet my seat. I am thankful. I hope that someone sees the wisdom beneath the folds in my eyelids. I still want to please. I remember Marie and realize that she genuinely wanted to help me. And I hope that those writing dreams survive until the stories are told. It is here that I abide a little bit longer.

… as life continues on …

This piece was in my heart and on my mind for several years before I finally took time to write it and post it as a blog on Labor Day of 2015. Although normally a more serious writer, I do enjoy making others and myself laugh. This piece was reflective but funny, and I love reading it even today. I should have pitched it to an office magazine.

Conclusion
Write On

I call myself a writer of real-life adventures and everyday life. I've also called myself a female *John-Boy*. For those of you too young to remember *The Waltons*, John-Boy was the main character in the popular television show that aired for ten years beginning in 1971. Each episode began with an older John-Boy narrating, setting the stage for the episode reflecting back on a time in his life growing up on Walton's Mountain in the 1930s. I absolutely loved the show and cried many times while watching.

WHY I WRITE

So why do I write, or cathart, as someone recently accused me? *(Well, cathart didn't pass spellcheck, but I knew what the person meant, so we'll go with it.)*

I don't want to give away the preface of my next book, so I will avoid explaining all of the details of when I first realized I wanted to write, but it was about twenty-five years ago. After attending a festival, an unction—a turning in my belly—surfaced and never went away. I wanted to write a book. I daydreamed about it for almost twenty years before I held my first book, *Reflections*. I did not have the concept for *Reflections* during those twenty years. I wasn't sure what my first book would be about, but the compulsion never went away.

Then, after a life changing event, the concept came. And one weekend while driving out of town with a friend to attend a Mom's weekend with our sons in college, I confided in my friend that my first book would be about people in my life, that each chapter would be titled with the person's name. It would be a time to remember the good things in people. It was a couple more years before I was able to finish the small book of vignettes, but at that moment, I had the concept and knew someday my dream would be a reality.

BLOGGING

I said I would *never* blog, but after attending a writing seminar in 2010, I started a blog as encouraged by the sponsor and other attendees of the writing workshop. They advised, "Write about what's going on in your life." The thought of exposing my thoughts and feelings on a regular basis seemed way out there for someone who is much more an introvert than an extrovert. However, it got easier over time, and I doubted too many people would find or read my material, so I wrote on.

I didn't (and don't) always write perfectly. I tend to write in a passive voice, and sometimes I misspell words that I have to correct later (or not) even though I re-read over and over again. That's why we have editors. Although I dreamed (and still do) of being able to write as an occupation, to make a living at it, in reality, it is more of a hobby and a passion of writing from my heart. But the dream still lives.

ENCOURAGEMENT AND CRITICISM

People who have read my books and blogs have been kind with their comments, family members and friends are encouraging, and my mother says everything I write is beautiful.

Soon after *Reflections* was published in 2011, I was invited to participate in a local writers' group. We shared pieces of our work and received feedback from each other. Although the critiques were not always pleasant, I learned to listen to what the other writers said and implemented some of their suggestions. We each had different styles and strengths, and I thank Marty and Erika specifically for their time and encouragement in pushing me to be a better writer. It was during these years that I had a few stories published in national magazines, and I give much of that credit to them. I am grateful to still see these ladies from time to time.

Last month, author Kristin Horvath came across one of my magazine stories and sent me a word of encouragement which came at a much-needed time. And then, within a week's time, I was caught off guard by a negative email. I have never received a negative comment on a blog or in a book review, neither have I ever received a scathing message in my author email account.

Well, I guess there's a first for everything.

The individual pointed out what was perceived as errors in my writing, was condescending throughout the message, attacked the very core purpose of *Reflections* (to remember the good things in people), and accused me of publicly shaming someone by taking a particular statement out of context and misinterpreting it. The person then focused in on a few personal threats if I wrote "such and such."

I had trouble processing these comments but had to deal with it internally. I chose not to respond and accepted that not everyone is going to like what I have to say. It has not been an easy task. Everyone is entitled to an opinion and to express that opinion if so inclined. I was inclined to defend but chose not to retaliate, not because I'm a better person. I simply decided to leave the person with their opinion and thoughts. But I had to decide what to do as a writer. Writing is not a game to me.

~ *Do I stop writing because of someone's negativity?*

~ *Do I stop doing the thing I have been compelled to do for twenty-five years when I finally see a bit of success?*

~ *Do I let someone squelch my dream?*

~ *Do I let one negative email trump or stay all of the positive, encouraging remarks?*

I think not. I am compelled to write.

As my cousin Jeanne might say: "WRITE ON!"

I think I will, and I think this could be the last chapter in my next book.

And, indeed, I *had* written the last chapter in my next book—this book, *Someday I Will Write*—first posted as a blog in October 2017. Thank you, again, for reading my stories. Now it's your turn to tell your stories. Your someday is today!

a time to be born and a time to die,
a time to plant and a time to uproot,
a time to kill and a time to heal,
a time to tear down and a time to build,
a time to weep and a time to laugh,
a time to mourn and a time to dance,
a time to scatter stones and a time to gather them,
a time to embrace and a time to refrain from embracing,
a time to search and a time to give up,
a time to keep and a time to throw away,
a time to tear and a time to mend,
a time to be silent and a time to speak,
a time to love and a time to hate,
a time for war and a time for peace.
What do workers gain from their toil?
I have seen the burden God has laid on the human race.
He has made everything beautiful in its time.
He has also set eternity in the human heart;
yet no one can fathom what God has done from beginning to end.

—Ecclesiastes 3:2-11

Credits

Bennard, George. "The Old Rugged Cross," 1913, Public Domain.

Bernard, Felix and Richard B. Smith. "Winter Wonderland," 1934, Warner Music Group.

Blackwell, Dewayne and Earl Bud Lee. "Friends in Low Places," *No Fences*, 1990, Capitol Nashville.

Brickman, Jim. "Simple Things," *Simple Things*, 2001, Windham Hill Records.

Buck, Chris and Jennifer Lee. *Frozen*. 2013; Burbank, CA: Walt Disney Studios Motion Pictures.

Butterfield, Daniel. "Taps," 1862, Public Domain.

Canfield, Jack and Mark Victor Hansen. *Chicken Soup for the Soul*. Deerfield Beach, FL: Health Communications, Inc., 1993.

Cukor, George. *Rich and Famous*. 1981; Beverly Hills, CA: Metro-Goldwyn-Mayer.

Debra Irene. *Reflections*. Bloomington, IN: WestBow Press, 2011.

Debra Irene. "So You've Always Wanted to Learn How to Golf?" *The Missouri Golf Post*, September 2013.

Debra Irene. "So You've Always Wanted to Play Golf, Part II." *The Missouri Golf Post*, July 2014.

Debra Irene. "Apple Butter Time." *Farm & Ranch Living*, August/
September 2014.

Debra Irene. "Stop and Pet the Pony." *Country*, August/September
2015.

Debra Irene. *Helen's Heritage: Life Stories of Helen Herbert Gillham
as Told to Debra Irene*. Bloomington, IN: WestBow Press, 2016.

Debra Irene. "Heart of a Home." *Country*, August/September
2016.

Debra Irene. "Handwritten Treasures." *Country Extra*, July 2017.

Dictionary.com. "vacation," accessed July 11, 2019, https://www.
dictionary.com/browse/vacation.

Gaither, Gloria and William J. Gaither. "There's Something About
That Name," 1970, William J. Gaither, Inc. ARR UBP of
Gaither Copyright Management.

Gaither, Gloria and William J. Gaither. "Because He Lives," 1971,
William J. Gaither, Inc. ARR UBP of Gaither Copyright
Management.

Haley, Alex. *Roots: The Saga of an American Family*. New York,
NY: Doubleday, 1976.

Horvath, Kristin. *From Heart to Hand: The Lost Art of a Written
Letter*. Bloomington, IN: Balboa Press, 2016.

Kenny G. "Songbird," *Duotones*, 1986, Arista Records, Inc.

Kenny G. "Winter Wonderland," *Miracles: The Holiday Album*,
1994, Arista Records, Inc.

Kenny G. "My Heart Will Go On (Love Theme from *Titanic*),"
1998, Arista Records, Inc.

Marxhausen, Joanne. *Some of My Best Friends Are Trees*. Art by
Benjamin Marxhausen. St. Louis, MO: Concordia Publishing
House, 1990.

Miles, C. Austin. "In the Garden," 1913, Public Domain.

Ortega, Fernando. "Give Me Jesus," *Home*, 2000, Word
Entertainment.

Pachelbel, Johann. "Canon in D," 1680, Public Domain.

"Party Like It's 1985 Royals Remix Video." YouTube video 2:50.
Posted by Bernstein-Rein, October 13, 2014. https://www.
youtube.com/watch?v=VE11h5qTgS8

Perry, Steve and Jonathan Cain and Neal Schon. "Don't Stop Believin'," *Escape*, 1981, Columbia.

Sanders, Mark D. and Tia Sillers. "I Hope You Dance," 2000, Universal—MCA Music Publishing.

Sommers, John Martin. "Thank God I'm a Country Boy," *Back Home Again*, 1974, RCA Records.

Stromberg, Robert. *Maleficent*. 2014; Burbank, CA: Walt Disney Studios Motion Pictures.

The Love Unlimited Orchestra. "Love's Theme," 1973, 20th Century Records.

Wallace, Randall. *Secretariat*. 2010; Burbank, CA: Walt Disney Studios Motion Pictures.

Williams, Paul and Roger Nichols. "We've Only Just Begun," 1970, Irving Music, Inc.

Acknowledgments

To God be the glory. Although I have missed the mark many times and in many ways throughout my lifetime, Jesus has covered me, and God has restored.

I am thankful for the ones closest to me for their encouragement over the years in my writing—Tim, my mother (Helen), and my sisters (Vickie, Kathy, Karin) and their husbands.

What a blessing it is to have a large extended family with so many heartwarming stories that have inspired my writing.

A few people who crossed my path and became "friends for life" encouraged me as I worked my day job and squeezed in times to write—Mary, Debbie, and Brenda. I miss my friend, Cathy, who first encouraged me to submit stories to magazines and is no longer here to celebrate the release of this book. Although my friend Cheryl didn't live to read any of my stories, I believe she is one in a great cloud of witnesses cheering me on.

Thanks, Marty and Erika, for those Sunday afternoons when we laughed, read, critiqued, ate, and drank. Our gatherings made me write even when I didn't feel like it. You made me a better teller of stories.

Honestly, I don't know how or why I remember so many things and am able to recount those things in such a way that resonates with others. That's why I say, "To God be the glory." I am grateful for every reader and every opportunity to share. Thank you for reading my stories.

About the Author

Debra Irene ... writer, storyteller, professional blogger, and author tells real-life stories as though she is speaking to a friend over a cup of coffee. Her portfolio is plump with by-lined features as a contributor to Trusted Media Brands family of magazines as well as specialty pieces featured in *The Missouri Golf Post*.

Her third book published in 2019, *Someday I Will Write*, is a collection of stories written over time when there appeared to be no time for her to write. The stories illuminate both the blessings and the heart-wrenching elements of human relationships and everyday life. In this book, aspiring writers can follow her journey and be encouraged to find time to tell their own stories. Previous titles include *Reflections* (2011), a series of original vignettes about family, friends, and faith. Next, *Helen's Heritage* (2016) chronicles her mother's journey, a depression-era child born the youngest of sixteen children who was separated from her mother before her second birthday.

An Executive Assistant for an entrepreneur and philanthropist by day and a dedicated author by night, she writes evenings, weekends, and whenever slivers of time allow. She loves speaking to groups of various sizes, inspiring them to embrace the seasons of life, keep walking, and tell their stories. She is active on Facebook, Twitter, and YouTube. Connect at DebraIrene.com.

The mother of three adult sons, Debra Irene lives in the metropolitan Kansas City area.